What to Do When "There's Nothing to Do"

BOSTON CHILDREN'S MEDICAL CENTER
AND ELIZABETH M. GREGG

Illustrated by Marc Simont

A DELL BOOK

Published by
Dell Publishing Co., Inc.
1 Dag Hammarskjold Plaza
New York, New York 10017

Portions of text previously published in the May, June, and July 1967 issues of *Woman's Day*.

Dell® TM 681510, Dell Publishing Co., Inc.

ISBN: 0-440-19471-7

Reprinted by arrangement with Delacorte Press/Seymour Lawrence
Printed in the United States of America

One Previous Dell Edition
New Dell Edition
First printing—October 1984

Contents

WHAT TO DO
WHEN
"There's Nothing to Do"

THE CHILDRENS MEDICAL CENTER · BOSTON 1869

Publications for Parents

This book is one of a series of *Publications for Parents,* a unique publishing program being carried on jointly by the Children's Hospital Medical Center of Boston and Dell Publishing Co., Inc. This new program marks the first time that a major medical center joins forces with a large publishing house to produce books and pamphlets for parents and children. The aim is to bridge the time gap between the emergence of a new medical development and its use by parents in day-to-day living.

Medical and psychological research and the experience of many physicians will provide the authoritative material for books, handbooks, and booklets on all phases of child growth and development. Pediatricians, surgeons, psychiatrists, social workers, and nursery-school teachers themselves, or writers working closely with them, will write the books. A medical review board of doctors from the hospital's staff will pass on each volume. An editorial office for this work has been established in the hospital's Department of Health Education, perhaps the only organization of its kind, whose sole task is to provide educational material for parents.

A Note About This Book

The idea for *What To Do When "There's Nothing To Do"* came from mothers who visit the Family Health Unit at the Boston Children's Hospital Medical Center. They bring their children for regular checkups and share with us their day-to-day problems. One question cropped up time and again. How does a mother keep young children happily and safely occupied when there's housework to be done or bad weather keeps them cooped up at home?

We decided to compile a list of play ideas for such occasions. We asked a Boston nursery-school teacher, Elizabeth Gregg, to write down some of her play "recipes" for a small pamphlet. Then other nursery-school teachers offered additional ideas. As hospital recreation workers, doctors, college child-study specialists, librarians and other experts in this field made their contributions, our original pamphlet turned into this full-length book.

As you try these suggestions, you probably will discover other "toys" and play ideas of your own. Please write us and tell us about them so we can add them to later editions of this book and make them available to other mothers, grandmothers and aunts.

We are especially grateful to: Joel J. Alpert, The Children's Hospital Medical Center, Boston; Marjorie E. Buell, Beacon Nursery School, Boston; Martha H. Chandler, Eliot Pearson Children's School, Tufts University; Louisa Cogswell, Lesley Ellis School, Cambridge; Dr. Thomas E. Cone, The Children's Hospital Medical Center, Boston; Dr. Leonard W. Cronkhite, Jr., The Children's Hospital Medical Center, Boston; Dr. Lydia Dawes, Beth Israel Hospital, Boston; Elsa S. Dorfman, Harvard Project Physics, Cambridge; Louise Ellison, Beacon Nursery School, Boston; Joan E. Erikson, Cambridge; Marilyn Goodman, The Children's Hospital Medical Center, Boston; Ethel Heins, *Hornbook Magazine*, Boston; Janet Loranger, Charles Scribner & Sons, New York; The Massachusetts Audubon Society; Barbara Patterson, The Children's Hospital Medical Center, Boston; Dr. Evelyn G. Pitcher, Eliot Pearson, Department of Child Study, Tufts University; Noni Reder, Eliot Pearson Children's School, Tufts University; and to Ruth E. Hartley and Robert M. Goldenson for permission to use several of the play suggestions in their book *Complete Book of Children's Play* (Thomas Y. Crowell, New York, 1963).

HARRIET H. GIBNEY
Director, Health Education
The Children's Hospital Medical Center

Introduction

This is much more than a book about play ideas for young children. It also reveals a fine understanding of children's behavior, and the way they develop and learn.

Beginning at infancy, the authors portray the limits as well as the potentials of each age through five. They are interested always in the child's achievements and ideas, and they emphasize that the most important aspect of the child's play is not the finished product but the doing.

This is not a "make-it" book although many of the suggestions for play involve making things. It is an approach to play that incorporates the dynamics of child development. The child's need to explore is understood, and his right to test, to experience and to wonder in freedom from regimentation is upheld. The book seeks to reinforce the psychologically constructive elements in play that the superficial observer may tend to dismiss as chaos or irrelevance.

The authors give the parents help in how to arrange

the environment so that the toddler, urged to move and discover his body in relation to space around him, can test his physical capacity, and develop awareness of himself. There are suggestions for providing the much-needed sensory experiences for heightening the child's awareness and responsiveness to the world around him. He may not use materials in the functional or practical ways he will later, but his "messing" has a purpose, and can be a step toward other important learning—vocabulary building, self-confidence, the joy of knowing.

There is imaginative play, too, with miniature objects, toys, or puppets, for the child's first ventures into what will be his social world. As he grows older and gains skills, he learns to master materials and create reproductions of what he sees adults make and do. Matching the activity to the stage of development has been the author's prime concern.

The book is, in a sense, a good text on child development, as well as a manual of helpful suggestions to parents about how they can enrich their child's play and their own daily home life.

EVELYN GOODENOUGH PITCHER
Chairman
Eliot-Pearson Department of Child Study
Tufts University
Medford, Massachusetts

WHAT TO DO
WHEN
"There's Nothing to Do"

ONE

What To Do When
"There's Nothing To Do"

What mother has never been confronted by that plaintive upturned face (or several of them), stating flatly, "There's nothing to do, Mommy, there's nothing to do"?

More often than not, the demand reaches its highest pitch on just those days when everything else is awry. The rain is pouring down. A mother is behind in her work, the supper still to be planned and cooked. She's tired and premenstrual and, wherever she turns, a discontented child is underfoot.

This book was started with just those days in mind. Children, especially preschool children, have an emotional radar for sensing a mother's flagging spirits and will go to all lengths to keep themselves at the center of her attention—just at the moment when she is fresh out of energy and ideas.

Sometimes, however, the complaint of nothing to do comes when a mother is feeling energetic and imaginative and inspired to create. So, as this book grew, we added play ideas for brighter days when mothers have a little extra time to do something with their children.

For the benefit of mothers, we chose ideas that would be practical, simple to set up, and usually would not require undivided attention or help. Mothers are not nursery school teachers and should not expect themselves to be; they have other things to do besides playing with their children. Most of the "toys" described in this book can be made from everyday materials which usually are on hand in any household and cost little or nothing. For what good would play ideas be to a busy mother if she had to drop everything to shop for special materials?

With the child's development foremost in mind, we have selected ideas to match as nearly as possible what is known about the particular needs and interests at different ages. Child specialists now seem to be concentrating their research on the very early years, particularly the first year of life, and before very long we will know much more than we do now about how children learn, how they develop mentally and what interests them most. Then we'll be able to add more play ideas to this book. In the meantime, our present knowledge of child development, while far from complete, is sufficient to let us be quite specific about certain matters.

In this book we have tried to give concrete answers to various important questions: What rests a baby? What interests him? When does he learn to grasp something and let it go? When do children stop throwing blocks and begin building with them? At what age is "messing around" with clay and mud especially valuable and why? When has a child enough coordination to use blunt scissors?

Until very recently, babies were overlooked as "players." What kept a baby happiest, it was thought, was food, cuddling and quiet. But now studies of early infants show that they are eager to play, and learn very quickly by touching, looking, listening. These activities are their "play." Their "toys" are simple but none the less important for being so. Research seems to be confirming the old idea that earliest childhood is the period of greatest learning.

Recognition that learning begins in the cradle does not require us, however, to bombard two-year-olds with first-grade primers or see how much of our adult knowledge we can thrust on a child as early as possible. The child's way of learning, about which we still have a great deal to discover, is different. His logic is not an adult's logic, his order not an adult's order, and he should have the freedom to learn in his own way. To some grown-ups, certain play ideas in this book may seem downright silly—tearing up newspapers, splashing water, or dumping cans on the floor. "Doing" is a child's way of experimenting with his world. It is not important to him to produce a "thing" in the adult sense. He needs the opportunity to use his own unique drive to master and to create.

A young child probably prefers "home" toys, such as pots and pans, cans and milk cartons, to store toys. These things are part of his daily life and he longs to reach out and experiment with them. Moreover, he sees his mother using them, so he wants to use them, too. "In the everyday experiences of the child," says Jean Piaget, the Swiss psychologist, "lie the origins of curiosity."

A baby's random movements and a child's seemingly aimless activities are his earliest methods of learning. A baby watching a mobile is exploring with his eyes. A two-year-old tearing papers, besides developing his hand coordination, is testing his mastery of his environment and satisfying his curiosity about materials. What do we mean when we say that an adult is creative? Only that his work exhibits the application of an unusual inventiveness to an unusual curiosity. There is a sense of play involved. The spirit of the backyard, mudpies, and lopsided structures of junk isn't very different from the spirit of a physics laboratory, an artist's studio, or an architect's drawing board.

Anyone who has closely watched a child at play quickly recognizes he is in the presence of hard work. Play is a child's work, and he approaches it earnestly. The toddler sits digging in the hard dirt with a metal spoon, scraping and scooping until the spoon strikes a large stone. He may spend an hour digging all around the stone with his spoon or he may get the garden trowel and solve his problem in five minutes. Basically, his task is the same as the problem-solving that confronts adults. They have to solve their problems in a more complex world, but the foundation of approaching and mastering problems often is laid on the problems of their childhood.

In play a child learns bit by bit what the world is— what is wet, what is dry, what hurts, what he can lift and push aside, what makes things stop and go, hold together, fall apart, and what jobs require calling for outside help. He experiments by feeling, smelling, tasting, dropping, kicking, messing, and watching. Play is also a good outlet for troubled feelings and overflowing energy. In games with other children, a child meets rage and attack, but also laughter and a sense of belonging. In play a child faces many of the crucial tasks of living. Just as his earliest relationships with his family color his attitudes in later life, so do his early play experiences, particularly his sense of fun.

All the play ideas in this book have been checked for safety by members of the staff of The Children's Hospital. In the hospital, we have a celebrated collection of objects that were removed from the stomachs or throats of small children, including safety pins, buttons, nails, hatpins, peanuts, cup hooks, jacks—and a collection of political campaign buttons from Roosevelt to Johnson. Our doctors have kept accidents very much in mind while checking over the list of play materials.

The "safest" home, however, has potential hazards and cannot be made truly safe even if it were desirable to make it so. As children grow, they must learn gradually to live with the hazards of everyday life. One of the chief dangers in play is that a young child will put things in his mouth. If it's sponge, it's all right. But, if it's a tack or a bottle of nail polish, beware. In the "three-, four- and five-year-olds" section we have used beans, buttons and dry macaroni and other small objects which are dangerous to give children who still chew everything. Most four-year-olds are no longer interested in putting these things in their mouths and can play with them safely. You will know whether or not you feel your child is safe playing with these things. If you're not sure, talk to your doctor about it.

CHOOSING WHAT TO DO WHEN

If the "nothing to do" day comes when you're exhausted and fresh out of ideas (or patience), consider your own capacities first. If you undertake a project that seems burdensome to you, it's almost certain that your child won't enjoy it much either. You may not want to do anything at all; in that case you might make each child a nutritious peanut butter sandwich and turn on TV. You can go to a nearby sofa and put your feet up. Forget about cooking supper. (But be sure your children are safe and you are where you can keep an eye on them.)

Useful as TV is, particularly around the supper hour, we don't recommend that you use it too much. Most

children's TV programs aren't very good yet (some are downright bad) and, even if they were, TV doesn't help a child to master his own skills.

There are many play ideas here on which your child, once you get him started, may play for a long time happily, all by himself. A three- or four-year-old can play safely in a nearby room with a cornmeal "sandbox" or stringing empty spools of thread. He won't need watching too closely. In the appendix under "Good Ideas When a Mother Is Out of Sorts," you will find a chart of other safe ideas that don't require close supervision.

When choosing a play idea, consider how your child is feeling, too. Is he tired? Is he overexcited? Is he feeling floppy? Or is he just plain bored? You will find in the appendix another chart, "Good Ideas for a Child Who Is Out of Sorts." This has some suggestions for the sick or tired child as well as for the child who needs to let off steam. It is good to remember that when a child (or an adult) is sick or tired, he likes to return to the simpler play of an earlier age. Don't give him anything too exacting.

It also helps to follow the lead of nursery school teachers in alternating quiet and active play periods. After a stint with crayons, which require great concentration and control of the hand and eye muscles, let your child have a good fight with crumpled newspaper "snowballs." A potato race might follow some stitching on cardboard.

Many mothers have asked how to keep children from fighting or fussing during that last difficult hour before supper, without constantly relying on TV. Card or board games almost inevitably lead to squabbling at this hour, when the children are too tired to put up with rules and regulations. A few suggestions might be: clay or play dough, pasting, some picture books from the library which you have put aside for this hour, a bag of light small blocks plus a few plastic animals or dolls from the dime store. In any case, choose something quiet that a child can do by himself, without your help or the participation of his brothers and sisters. Friendly brotherly-sisterly participation rarely occurs in that hour before supper. But a little diversion at this crucial time of day can work miracles.

Although we have tried in this book to list play ideas according to chronological age, this has been a difficult job because no two children develop exactly in step. Some toilet train themselves early, others later. Some two-year-olds have early hand-eye coordination, others are particularly attuned to music. Some stop putting things in their mouths at two, others not until five. You will know your own child and what he likes to do. If you see a game or toy listed for four-year-olds which might appeal to your two-year-old, or if he loves an activity in the baby section, let him enjoy it to his heart's content—if it's safe. But above all, don't worry if your three-year-old finds most of his fun in the toddler section. He'll learn soon enough. Pushing may only frustrate and discourage him.

The secret of successful play is choosing the activity which best suits your needs and those of your child at the moment. Playing with water in the kitchen sink, for instance, is a good activity when you must be working in the kitchen anyway. A visit to a food factory or to the florist might be fun on a day when you want to get out of the house and forget it.

On the other hand, if it's raining and your child has just fallen down and scraped his knee, and moreover has a case of the sniffles and is at odds with his brothers and sisters, it may be that he doesn't want to do anything at all. He may just want to sit in your lap and have you talk to him. Sometimes a song is good, too.

STARTING AND STOPPING

Almost every child needs help getting started—even if he's playing with something familiar that he can do by himself. After you have set out the materials, play with him for four or five minutes to help him get involved. Don't tower over him but sit down beside him or join him on the floor and show him how. Your own enthusiasm and fun will do a lot to interest him.

Before stopping play, give a child five or ten minutes warning to let him have time to finish what he's doing. If he's really involved and doesn't want to stop, be firm but talk about what he can do the next time he plays with these materials. It's important for play to end happily and for a child to realize that he can pick up at another time where he left off today.

And don't forget to praise a child for what he is able to do. The stagger on stilts, the lumpy piece of clay or the drippy mudpie are, in a very real sense, masterpieces. Children feel very proud to have their art work tacked up on the wall or shown to their fathers when they come home. Then the "nothing to do" day suddenly turns into a day of triumph.

TWO

Babies

Although he sleeps a good part of each day, a baby will grow faster and change more during the first year of life than at any other age. His growth is fostered by his daily experiences with the world that immediately surrounds him. By touching things he learns where his body ends and the world begins. He learns to tell one sound from another by listening. He trains his eyes to focus by shifting them. Small objects help teach him how to grasp and how to let go. At the center of this world is his mother and, without the loving attention of a single devoted person, he would have grave difficulty growing at all. A mother and child's moments of play and pleasure together are the foundation of a baby's learning.

But no two babies are quite the same. Right from birth they seem to have distinct personalities and preferences. Some are cuddlers and love being held, patted and snuggled. Others are not so keen on cuddling and may even tense up or rear back if held closely. Some are restless and wakeful; others are placid and sleep a lot. Some love to be uncovered; others hate it. Some love sounds; others don't. But, in some way or other, all babies need lots of loving care. Look for the clues which indicate your baby's special needs and pleasures. It is his developing relationship with you that will encourage him to drink in new sights, sounds and sensations, to grow and learn new things.

The best time for play is when you both feel like it. It's hard for you to play if you're dead tired and it's hard for him if he's hungry or sleepy. But there is no sense to the old rule that a baby must be kept quiet and put to sleep after a feeding, or that he shouldn't be bathed until he has digested his food. Some babies may spit up a little if handled roughly after a feeding, but the value of the play far outweighs such a minor loss. In fact, the period surrounding both bathing and feeding times can be especially good play times.

Nor is it necessary to take a small baby outdoors every day. If you feel like going out and want to take the baby with you, by all means do, but he won't suffer by staying indoors.

The following play ideas are not all new. Many have been handed down by mothers through the centuries, but they are all supported by scientific research into how a baby learns. Pick out an activity that seems to suit you and your baby best at any particular moment. If your baby obviously doesn't enjoy it, try something else; the same criterion holds for you as much as you can, do what you both enjoy doing, when you both feel like it.

UNDER THREE MONTHS

Touching: A baby's sense of touch is highly developed and he may learn more through touching and being touched than in any other way.

If your baby likes being held, there's nothing like the rocking chair. Motion and touch are combined plus comfort for mothers as well as babies. If you hold your baby on your shoulder as you rock, he may enjoy exploring your face with his fingers as he grows a little older. If you hold him in your arms or on your lap, he will grasp one of your fingers if you put it in his hand. (Babies can grasp at birth. This is an inborn reflex, not a conscious action on his part.)

When he's awake, take him with you from room to room (see looking chair, p. 34) so he can see and hear you while you work. Some mothers carry their babies around both inside the house and out in papoose boards, or specially designed packsacks. So long as they are in a comfortable position, most babies like this closeness to their mothers and the motion of their bodies. Keep in touch with your baby through many senses—sight, sound and feel.

To quiet a crying baby, try wrapping him (fairly firmly) from the waist down in a receiving blanket. Leave his arms free. The quieting effect of this kind of bundling is well known by peoples in other cultures who swaddle their babies a good deal of the time. They feel it gives the child a feeling of being held securely in his mother's arms. Another way to quiet a crying baby is a variation on swaddling: put your hand fairly firmly on his stomach or gently hold one of his arms or legs. This seems to have a quieting effect, especially if a baby is startled.

Listening: From birth, babies are sensitive to sound and especially to high frequencies. As you bathe or dress or feed your baby, sing, hum or whistle a tune you like. If you hit a few flat notes, your child will never notice. You may never have a more appreciative audience! For him, no disembodied voice coming from

a machine can ever replace his own mother's singing. Babies seem to be able to hear rather high-pitched sounds best and usually react more quickly to a woman's voice than to a man's. This may be the reason that "baby talk" is usually high pitched. However, a man's voice or a lower-pitched mixture of sounds such as those of an orchestra seem to be more soothing and more effective in lulling a child to sleep.

When you are not with your child, the gentle sound of a small clock ticking next to his crib or of a radio playing soft music may comfort him. A wind chime hung near his window where the breeze will catch it can be particularly soothing.

Looking: A tiny baby spends most of his time lying down. His eyes are often focused upon the ceiling, the upper parts of the walls, and the sides of his crib. You can make these blank areas more interesting by hanging posters and pictures on the walls or fastening strips of colored oilcloth on the inside of the crib. Bright colors that contrast with the background seem to be best. Strong reds and yellows seem to be particularly appealing.

Crib Mobile: Don't worry that your baby will grab any of these things and put them in his mouth. He won't do this until he's about three months old. But keep the trinkets high enough so they won't touch him if he turns over. Take a thin wooden rod such as a balloon stick or a thin bamboo plant stake and tie it across the width of the crib. With scotch tape or a bit of string, fasten onto it some of these things:

> old costume jewelry
> crumpled pieces of aluminum foil
> colored plastic measuring spoons
> bright paper cut into spirals, squares or circles
> bits of bright cloth

Or, if you have a ceiling fixture, tie a string around it and fasten a wire coat hanger to the bottom end of the string. From the hanger, tie on different lengths of string or thread and attach some of these articles to the strings.

More Sights: Babies often enjoy looking at lights. If your baby seems fussy, put a lighted lamp (with a shade) where he can look at it without hurting his eyes. Or set a small colored glass vase or drinking glass on the window ledge for the sun to shine through. Moving a fretful child to a different room will sometimes quiet him by giving him new things to look at.

The Looking Chair: Babies love to watch other children at play or their mothers busy with household chores. It is well worth spending a few dollars for an infant seat so that your baby can be part of the family activity. It's easy to carry him from room to room in this chair and he can also see what's going on without straining his back or head. (Be sure the safety belt is fastened so he can't fall out.) If you put him on a kitchen table, bed or sofa, be sure that he is in the middle of it, in case he manages to tip the seat over. This rarely happens, even with an active infant, but it makes sense to be careful.

A baby often likes to be in the center of action. Try strapping him into his infant seat and putting the seat in the middle of an empty playpen. The other children can then play outside the pen. The baby will be at their level to watch their movements and hear their chatter. He will also be somewhat protected from their attentions. But since they can still hurl toys at the baby or climb into the pen with him, be sure to keep a watchful eye.

Don't leave the baby alone in the room with other children.

Bath Time: Some young babies can be upset by baths. They don't seem to like that naked, exposed feeling and are sometimes startled by their own arm and leg movements. If your baby reacts this way, try wrapping him in a diaper or receiving blanket before placing him in the water. Usually, after he is dunked he will stop crying and you can remove the covering. (This is how women in India keep their babies happy in the bath.) Or, try gently holding his arm after he is undressed so that he doesn't thrash so freely. This is often reassuring.

THREE TO SIX MONTHS

Cradle Gym: As soon as a baby learns to reach and grasp (somewhere around four or five months), a mobile must be raised to a safe distance where he can't reach any fragile or possibly dangerous objects. Instead of a mobile, make a simple cradle gym with safe, smooth objects he can play with. Tie a length of heavy-gauge elastic stripping across the crib, and attach short lengths of thinner elastic strips to it. Then, tie on two or three of these:

> an empty spool of thread
> smooth plastic spoons
> a large bell
> a smooth plastic bracelet
> a rattle
> other smooth-surfaced toys too large for him to swallow

Try this on the baby carriage, too.

Squeeze Toys: Pieces of worn toweling or oilcloth can be sewed together and stuffed with old nylon stockings. Babies this age prefer vivid colors of red, yellow, orange and purple to the more traditional pale pink and blue. Stuffed toys don't have to be teddy bears and dolls; a doughnut shape is easier for small hands to pick up.

Bounce Chair: This is a good time to buy a bounce chair, sometimes called a "stationary jumper"—a chair built on a metal frame with a plastic or canvas sling seat, with two holes in the front for the baby's legs. It allows the baby to sit up and bounce and, at the same time, protects the lower part of his back from strain.

Sometimes a baby of five or six months will bounce around too much and act a little groggy from so much motion. If your child seems floppy in his chair, try tying the back of it to its metal stand on the floor. This stabilizes the chair somewhat and keeps him from falling forward. It gives him support similar to the infant seat.

Playpen Toys: Around four months, many babies start to spend time in a playpen. Some household items they enjoy holding or chewing are:

> a smooth clothespin—the old-fashioned kind, not the springy, pinching type
> a sponge
> large empty spools—tie four or five on a string
> a smooth plastic bracelet
> a rattle
> other smooth-surfaced toys too large for him to swallow

Games to Play: At about four or five months, most babies like being carried to a mirror to see themselves and their mothers or fathers. If you ask "Who is it?" or "What is that?", they are mystified and usually delighted. This is the age, too, when babies begin to learn to control parts of their bodies in simple movements, like nodding their heads or sticking out their tongues. Try nodding your head and see if he imitates you. Or make a clucking noise and see if he responds with one of his own. "Oh" is a simple word he may like to imitate.

Babies this age are also amused by hearing a sudden change in pitch in someone's voice, from high to low and back again. Try playing back and forth with your baby using these simple sounds and movements.

Bath Time: As he grows older, a baby usually is fascinated with water. When he enjoys sitting up in the bath, support his back and let him spend a few minutes splashing with his hand or kicking his feet. By this age, he probably won't want his bath wrapping any longer.

SIX TO NINE MONTHS

As a baby begins to sleep less, he begins to be able to play happily by himself for perhaps half an hour at a time. But he also wants to watch you while he plays.

This is the age for dropping and throwing things, for he is just learning how to let go of objects and he likes to experiment with his new knowledge. Spare yourself a lot of stooping and bending by tying toys to his bounce chair or stroller. Put them on short strings or shoelaces and he can drop and then retrieve them by pulling up the string. Try:

> a metal cup with handle
> small metal pie tins (aluminum frozen-food
>   and TV-dinner tins are ideal; make a hole
>   for the string)
> pie lids (tie the string to the handles)
> color-fast ribbons
> wooden spoon (to bang)
> small juice cans (with a hole punched in
>   end for stringing; make sure the hole is too
>   small for a tiny finger and that edges are
>   smooth)
> small empty cardboard gift boxes
> adhesive-bandage cans
> old reels from cellophane or adhesive tape

In his playpen, he will push these things through the slats or throw everything out on the floor. Tie them to the playpen with short strings.

Bounce Chair: If you've tied the bounce chair (see p. 35), your baby is probably now ready to bounce more freely. Try removing the stabilizing string and see if he enjoys the more energetic movement.

Nesting Toys: Around the age of seven months, a baby begins to discover how to put one thing inside of another. He really isn't ready yet for square nesting toys, but a variety of round empty metal cans will amuse him. Start with the small frozen orange-juice size (be sure there are no sharp edges from the can opener) and add other soup and vegetable cans of different sizes.

Games: A baby this age loves to play with people he knows. When he is feeling sociable, try some of the time-honored, well-loved nursery games. A child six months old usually likes to be swung gently back and forth. Hold him firmly with both your hands under his armpits. Your child may also enjoy riding cock-horse on someone's knee and being passed from one well-loved person to the next. Some time around nine months he will be able to connect words with actions. He'll like "Pat-a-cake," "This little pig went to market" (wiggle his toes while you say it), and "Peek-a-boo." He'll usually respond to "bye-bye" by waving his hand.

Feeding Fun: At his age, feeding time can become a wonderful play time. As your baby becomes more interested in the spoon or cup, give him an extra one to bang with while you feed him with the other. As he gets more independent and less interested in your feeding him, give him some soft bits of bread or banana to pick up and put in his mouth by himself. While he's occupied with his own work, you can keep spooning the messier foods into his mouth. In this way, you encourage his growing ability to feed himself and keep alive his interest in food.

Water Play: When a baby learns to grasp and let go, he loves playing with a sponge or washcloth in the bath. He can squeeze the sponge or suck it. It's all right for him to put it in his mouth. The bath water won't hurt him.

THREE

Toddlers and Crawlers

Sometime around eight months a baby starts to crawl and, soon after (between ten and twelve months), to pull himself to his feet by the side of his playpen. Before you know it, he has begun to toddle, and to toddle with amazing speed. Some babies crawl for a long time, others walk without doing much crawling first. Whether he's a crawler or a toddler, he'll gain experience quickly and then move about very fast.

Urged forward by his new sense of mobility, he is apt to become an undaunted explorer, with all the zeal but with none of the sense of danger of his grown-up counterpart. If not watched carefully, he'll run into a busy street, climb a ladder or try tasting the bleach underneath the kitchen sink.

THIS IS THE ACCIDENT AGE

It doesn't do much good to warn or scold ("No! No!", "Don't touch that!") or punish a child this age because he often can't understand the danger. Even if he does, his memory is short and he probably won't be able to remember your warning from one half hour to the next.

It's much safer and more relaxing to "toddler proof" your house. Remove to a safe height all dangerous objects or things you treasure. Cover any unused electric outlets with plastic covers (available at any local hardware store). Be sure all medicines (especially candy-flavored aspirin) are kept well out of his reach. Even if he crawls on top of the bathroom sink (as many children do), he should not be able to reach medicine. Remove cleaning products—such as ammonia or furniture polish—from beneath the kitchen sink. Toddlers love to put everything in their mouths and are apt to eat or drink anything. They have been known to down half a can of kerosene without minding the taste.

Outdoors, unless you have a safe and fenced-in yard, a toddler or crawler must be watched closely. Many mothers have been surprised by the quick-as-lightning speed of a child who, just a week or two before, only sat placidly waving his rattle.

While requiring close supervision, a toddler needs lots of opportunities to try things on his own. He loves to "do" and by "doing" he builds up his confidence and his abilities.

With toys, his insatiable curiosity is a blessing. Although he's not likely to play with any one thing very long (and you shouldn't expect him to), he is pleased with anything new, from a rolled-up piece of paper to an empty Jello box.

He loves hiding behind a chair or door and having some grown-up ask, "Where's baby?" He likes to have you hand him something so he can hand it right back to you. He loves it if his father swings him high in the air. He wants to be cuddled and sung to by his mother.

When a baby learns to walk, he suddenly has a new view of the world. He used to look up at the undersides of tables and chairs. People seemed as big as giants. Now he can see the tops of chairs and his view of grown-ups starts at their knees. Overnight his new perspective and his urge to explore make a playpen seem far too restrictive, and he may object (sometimes rather loudly) to being left to play in it.

On the other hand, you may have other things to do and don't want to keep running after him. At such times try using a "furniture playpen" (see below) and give him a few of the household items described on the following pages which are safe for him to play

with without supervision. From time to time, join him in his space to start him off on a new game. Toddlers learn by imitation and it is usually necessary to engage their interest in a new activity by doing it with them for a few minutes first.

A FURNITURE PLAYPEN WITH SIMPLE TOYS

To make a furniture playpen, section off a fair-sized space in the corner of a room (away from electrical outlets), with sofa and chairs and a suitcase or two. If your child can see you, he should be happier here than in a playpen. And this will save you from running after him and worrying about what he's up to.

In this playpen (or elsewhere) see how he likes to play with some of these toys:

wooden spoons   (p. 38)   small metal pie tins
nesting cans   (p. 39)   (p. 38)
squeeze toys   (p. 35)

A Wastebasket of Discarded Letters: He will keep engrossed for a long time pulling the stuff out. You'll have to put it back in again! (Be sure there is nothing harmful such as paper clips or glass in the basket.)

Line up old-fashioned clothespins along the edge of a loaf pan. After you have set them up, show him how to pull them off and drop them into the pan. The game is even more fun if you line them up all over again.

Pots and Lids: Lots of noise, but lots of fun, too! For variety, hide some safe object like an orange juice can in a pot and let the toddler find it by "surprise" when he takes the lid off.

Metal Coffee Percolator: A toddler will love its various parts, fitting them together and then taking them apart again. For safety, remove the glass piece from the lid if it has one.

Empty Milk Cartons: Save pint- and quart-size waxed milk cartons with flat tops (or cut off the tops of peaked ones). Soon you'll have a good set of blocks for a child eighteen months or older. He will enjoy moving one around (with both hands) but will rarely start stacking or throwing the cartons until he's about two and a half.

Empty Oatmeal Boxes: Good to push and roll.

Large Scraps of Brightly Colored Silk Ribbon, Velvet or Synthetic Fur Fabrics: are fun to feel and chew. Tie some of these to his playpen or stroller. Be sure they are made of colorfast materials.

Empty Gift Boxes, Jar Lids, Soap Wrappers: intrigue a one-year-old more than a store-bought toy.

A Shoe or Oatmeal Mailbox: Cut a large round hole in the lid of a shoe box or oatmeal cylinder. Show him how to drop empty thread spools or small blocks into it and dump them out again by taking off the lid.

Scribbling: Give him a large sheet of brown wrapping paper or a newspaper. Or take a large paper bag, tear it open so that it's flat, and tape the ends down to the floor or table so that it won't slide. Then hand a toddler two or three sturdy crayons and show him how to scribble. (Let him work on a surface which won't be damaged by crayon marks.)

PULL TOYS

A toddler likes to pull practically anything attached to the end of a string or rope. Choose something that doesn't weigh very much so that it won't bang the furniture. It shouldn't be able to splinter or crack either, since it might hurt the child. The most successful kind of pull toy should produce some sound when it is dragged around. So look through the house for articles which are light-weight, unbreakable, and not *too* noisy (for your sake). Some good pull toys are:

an old metal measuring cup

old bracelets (wooden, heavy plastic or metal)

empty spools (thread, typewriter or film)

toilet paper or towel tubes

pine cones

old stuffed animals

ice-cream cylinder carton

small boxes

hair rollers

wooden spoons

metal jar caps (punch a tiny hole through the center of the lid with a nail)

You can put two or three of these on the same string. Be sure to knot each object a few inches apart.

To make a *train*, attach several ice-cream cartons or small boxes. To make a *centipede*, alternate metal jar caps and empty spools. Hair rollers strung end-to-end would make a marvelous worm.

Round Ice-Cream Carton: Run a string through the carton from the lid to the bottom and secure it with a knot so it can be pulled around. Put in a handful of dry macaroni and tape the top on securely. This will make a lively noise when a child pulls or shakes it.

Empty Shoe Boxes: strung together with strong string, make trains, cars, boats.

KITCHEN PLAY

After a baby passes his first birthday, the kitchen becomes a more and more fascinating world, but he must be watched with an eagle eye to see that he doesn't get into the wrong places. The kitchen can be the most dangerous room in the house. For safety and long-time entertainment, you might try:

The Reserved Kitchen Drawer: Set aside a low drawer, or shelf, and fill it with old beat-up pots and pans, pie plates, covers, empty cans, a percolator, tea-spoons, and wooden spoons. If you can't spare an extra shelf or drawer, use a cardboard carton. While you are working in the kitchen, your child has his special drawer (or carton) with his own cooking toys.

CLIMBING AND CRAWLING

A Table Leaf and Cardboard Cartons: Support both ends of a table leaf or small wood plank with two small cartons—or a couple of large telephone books—to raise it about eight inches off the floor. A small child will like crawling over his bridge.

Big Grocery Cartons: Cut out both ends of two or three cartons. Turn them over and line them up, and he has a tunnel.

Throw *a blanket* over a small table (a card table is ideal) and tie it on with a circle of rope. This makes a wonderful house and a good place to play peek-a-boo. Children like to play under tables or behind a sofa or big chair.

WATER GAMES, INDOORS AND OUT

Outdoors: If you're lucky enough to have a yard, even if it's only a bare patch of dirt, you have what your toddler enjoys playing with the most—dirt, sand and water. An old tire makes a good sandbox but it isn't necessary to have any box at all. Most one-year-olds ignore the box anyway, and dump and strew the sand everywhere.

Just a small pile of sand (of the coarsest, cheapest kind), some loose gravel and a pile of dirt will keep a small child happy for a long, long time. Give him a stick or spoon to dig with and a pan or small bucket of water. Sand-play tools from the store don't work as well as big metal or wooden spoons. Large plastic bleach or starch containers with their tops cut off are ideal containers. An old sieve, collander or garbage strainer from your kitchen is fine for sifting.

A toddler spends so much of his day being washed and changed that he usually loves having one spot where he can be as messy as he wants. For yard playing, dress him in old things you don't care about, and then he can stir, dip and splatter all he wishes.

Indoors: Water is one of the most wonderful playthings a child can have. It has one major disadvantage for mothers, however. It is wet. The most convenient arrangement for water play indoors is to put your child into a dry bathtub in old clothes (or naked, if it's warm enough) and give him a pan of water. (Or, if it's easier for you, just draw a shallow bath.) There he can splash to his heart's content while you clean the bathroom or set your hair. (Be sure to stay in the bathroom with him.)

Give him some empty spools and small pieces of wood. He can make the spools "ride" on wood "boats." Tightly capped, empty plastic bottles also float and are fun. So are soft soap flakes (and perhaps some water softener) for billows of bubbles. A laundry sprinkler is good for squeezing and squirting.

MUSIC AND DANCING

Some children love music, others aren't so keen. But, for those who do, music—quiet or active—can be wonderfully restorative. Highly active or high-strung children often drift off to sleep more easily when listening to a lullaby or even more rhythmic music like jazz and rock 'n' roll. Don't overlook classical music.

For an "activity" record, Pete Seeger or Burl Ives folksongs send toddlers happily bobbing around the room in time to the music. Many children fall in love with Mother Goose songs at this age and continue to cherish them for years.

In the "Children's Records" section (pp. 167–172) there is a list of folksongs, nursery rhymes set to music, and classical music. You will also find a list of books (p. 172) filled with songs that children have loved for generations. See if your local library has copies of either the songbooks or the records.

RHYMES AND READING

Even without music, babies this age like little rhymes and rhythms—like "Pat-a-cake" or "Jack-be-nimble." They like to associate words with movements. If it's something you would do naturally, try reciting some nursery rhymes when you take him for a walk, change his diapers or put him in the playpen. Although a baby can't carry on a conversation, he loves the rhythm of someone else's words.

A good book can often capture the imagination of a child for a long time—sometimes from babyhood until the fourth grade. This is because children love familiar things, so that the same book, such as *Mother Goose* or *Little Fur Family* (See pp. 156–157), can be used in a variety of ways. Where a one-year-old may enjoy hearing you read aloud to him, a fifteen-month-old child, who can sit comfortably in your lap, may like to do his own reading by naming the pictures. It's fun for him just to be able to point to the objects he knows and tell you what they are—"dog," "ball," "tree," "Daddy," "house."

In choosing a book for a toddler, it's a good idea to find one with very bright colors, even if they seem garish to you. This is because his eyes are not yet tuned to subtle hues or pastel shades, like pale pink, blue or yellow.

You can also make a fine book for a toddler yourself. Try:

Picture Cards (without words). Cut cardboard into 5-inch-by-8-inch cards and paste on each one a large, brightly colored picture of something familiar, like a truck or cat or dog. The more realistic and sharply defined the picture, the better. The 5-inch-by-8-inch card is just the right size for an eighteen-month-old child to hold and focus his eyes upon. He may talk to himself about each picture, repeating the word over and over.

On the other hand, he may not be at all interested in having you read aloud to him or in looking at pictures. Don't press him or he may take an active dislike to the whole business. He'll take to books soon enough. Try again in a few months' time.

FOUR

For All Ages:
A Surprise and Comfort Bag

There are always those special occasions—the long waits at the dentist's or sick in bed at home—when a child must amuse himself quietly. These can be restless times for both mother and child. A "surprise and comfort bag," filled with new toys and hidden away for special occasions, can often save the day. You will find it useful for:

> Trips to the doctor or dentist or hospital which sometimes involve long, boring periods of waiting without play materials in the reception room.
> Trips to the beauty parlor, airport, or train station when you must take your small child with you.
> Airplane, train or long car trips.
> Trips to Grandmother's or to other households where there are no other young children and few toys around.

Sickbed days, when the surprise bag can be hung over your child's bedpost or pinned to the bedsheets at the side of the bed for easy reaching.

To make a surprise and comfort bag: a paper shopping bag is ideal. Write your child's name on the outside with a marking pencil and then shellac the bag inside

and out to make it waterproof and more durable. Or, use an airline's tote bag or a plastic-coated shopping bag. Manila envelopes of various sizes may be stapled to the inside of the bag to keep the contents from becoming a jumble. Into one of these, tuck a few Jiffy towels or wash 'n' dry packets. They'll be useful for sticky faces and fingers.

It's best to have a special bag for each child.

What to Put In: Keep the surprise bag filled and ready for service. You may want it in a hurry. It isn't necessary to buy anything; if your child hasn't seen an old toy for a while, it will seem new to him. An old pocketbook filled with junk is fun, and so are sheets of unused Christmas or Easter seals to stick on blank paper. A half-used roll of scotch tape and some scraps of colored construction paper and scissors can often occupy a child for a long time, or an old pack of playing cards to sort. What you keep in the bag obviously depends on your child's age and his special interest. It is best, however, to avoid noisy toys or things that roll away or which might annoy other people. Dry finger foods like cereal or raisins are good, but chocolate smears and soft fruits get squashed. When you are shopping, keep an eye open for little surprises that you can add to the bag.

Some good things for the surprise bag:

playing cards (for sorting and building)
bean bag
flannel board and scraps of flannel
wooden cheese boxes with lids, and some-
old pocketbook with old keys, costume jewelry, handkerchief, etc.
sewing cards and yarn (unsafe for travel)
magnifying glass

thing inside (empty walnut shells, for instance)

pipe cleaners

magic markers (washable)

thick crayons and pad of paper

blunt scissors

scotch tape

magnet

miniature doll family

small animals and cars

pick-up sticks (unsafe for travel)

gummed labels, stamps and paper shapes, stars, moon, etc.

colored construction paper

magic slate

coloring book

doctor or nurse kit

small boxes of raisins and dry cereal

"Comfort Toys": If you are going out, be sure to slip in one or two of your child's favorite and familiar toys just before you leave. At each age, a child will cling to some toys which he especially cherishes—a teddy bear, an old blanket. In a strange or unsettling circumstance, these familiar things are especially comforting for they are the child's link with home. These are the "comfort toys."

The Surprise Bag at Home: If your child is sad or seems "at loose ends," pick out one toy that might seem new and special. This often saves a blue day. Or, if you are leaving him with a new baby sitter, let him close his eyes and dip into the bag for a "surprise." If he is sick in bed, pin the whole bag to the side of the bed but keep only a few toys in it at a time. You can exchange toys as the day goes on, thus producing new "surprises" throughout the day.

FIVE

Two- and Three-Year-Olds

The child from two to three loves familiar beat-up toys. He usually has a ragged piece of blanket or an old stuffed toy he takes everywhere with him. He doesn't really play with other children yet; he may hug or poke or else totally ignore them. He isn't a sharer of toys, for he wants to keep his own special treasures to himself. Let him do this and have plenty on hand for the other children. He'll grow to be more sociable when he's three or older.

All young children differ from one another in developing their muscular skill and social abilities. Some become skillful with their hands easily; others may instead be training their ears or eyes. For this reason, we have called this chapter "Two- and Three-Year-Olds" and the next chapter, "Three-, Four- and Five-Year-Olds." Most of the ideas in the next section are for older three-year-olds, but your child may have developed a special ability in hand-eye coordination, for instance, and might want to try something in the next section. Just be sure it's safe. Remember, too, that when they are tired or sick, children prefer the simpler play of earlier ages.

Many a two-year-old's favorite word is "no." He's just beginning to assert himself and this means testing his will and yours. It can be exasperating, but if he weren't negative at times, he wouldn't be developing.

Often, if you don't make an issue of it, you can simply ignore his protest. Sometimes he really means "no." Then it's best to distract him. Fortunately, he can be distracted quite easily, especially if you let him make his own choices. If he is feeling very negative, it often works better to show him two objects, and when he reaches for one, rapidly remove the other. If you ask him, "Do you want the blue crayon or the purple one?" he may get completely hung-up over the choice.

This is the age, too, when a child is apt to be preoccupied with his bowel movements. That is one rea-

son why a two-year-old finds wet and gooey substances so fascinating. With other toys, his attention span is very fleeting, but if you give him a pan of water and some sand or mud, he'll probably play for a long time.

Play ideas the two-year-old still enjoys:

WATER PLAY

If you're working in the kitchen, let your child stand on a sturdy chair and use a dishpan in the sink. Spread newspapers on the floor to soak up the drippings and protect his clothes with a plastic apron. (Make a poncho by cutting a round hole in the middle of an old plastic crib sheet or tablecloth and pull it over the child's head.) Keep this home-made poncho in place by tying a heavy string around his waist. Or, all else failing, let him wear his bathing suit on a hot day.

Mothers aren't always keen about having their children play with water in the house except in the kitchen or bath. But, if you must be busy in some other room and your child wants to join you, you can waterproof any small area by spreading an old shower curtain or plastic tablecloth on the floor and covering it with a thick layer of newspapers. Set a small dishpan half full of warm water in the middle.

For the kitchen sink or the living room dishpan, here is a fine collection of toys:

funnel	plastic baster or laundry
measuring spoons	dampener
and cups	plastic squeeze bottle
handkerchiefs or doll	(empty)
clothes (to wash)	piece of floating soap
muffin tin	sponge
juice cans	plastic ice-cream
sieve	containers
small plastic pitcher	

For more fun, add a few drops of food coloring and some liquid detergent to the water. Let him stir them in.

Soap Bubbles: Give your child a plastic drinking straw and a cup (or empty juice can) filled with soap flakes and water. Children two and a half years and older can learn to blow, not suck, if you show them how. Since the cup is bound to overflow, it is best to use a tray under it. To make bubbles tough enough to float in the air without breaking, add a tiny bit of cooking oil to the soap-and-water mixture. The bathtub and outdoors are good places for soap bubbles.

CLAY PLAY

Children between two and three love to play with something they can pound and squeeze, break apart and put together again. Tearing and pounding give them an opportunity to express feelings they are not yet able to put into words. A fretful child will often be much calmer and happier after a good pounding session with clay.

All the ingredients for clay are right in your kitchen.

Play Dough:

> 1 cup salt
> 1½ cups flour
> ½ cup water
> 2 tablespoons oil
> a few drops of food coloring (optional)

This dough lasts for weeks if you store it in the refrigerator in a plastic bag or a covered jar. Children can pull and pound it, and then it can be collected and put away for another day, or they can make "things" and leave them out to dry and harden. (Small children may put this dough in their mouths. It won't taste good, but it won't hurt them.) Let your child sit at the kitchen table or on the floor, using a cookie sheet for a working space. Dust his hands with a little flour so the dough won't stick to his fingers. He may just want to pound and squash the dough with his hands. Or he might have fun with:

> a rolling pin
> cookie cutters
> dull knives, forks, and spoons

PASTING

Children usually don't paste very well until they are three or older, but younger ones love to mess with it. Some mothers give their two-year-olds a pat of vaseline or cold cream to smear over a cookie sheet and they have a dandy time making swirly patterns. This may seem a strange idea, but, actually the vaseline or cream is easier to wash off than mud; and it helps some small children who have a great urge to be messy become more cooperative. If they put a little in their mouths, it won't hurt them. (Naturally, you will have to watch

and see that they don't start smearing the stuff on the walls and furniture.)

Or try this recipe for homemade no-cook paste:

a handful of flour
add water (a little at a time) until gooey
    (it should be quite thick, so it won't run all
    over the paper)
add a pinch of salt

This no-cook paste is not so sticky as boiled paste (p. 88), but if you haven't the time or the facilities to cook, this paste holds scraps of paper together pretty well. Although it doesn't taste delicious, it won't hurt a child if he puts some in his mouth. Your child may be happiest just smearing this paste on a cookie sheet. Or he may like to try sticking scraps of paper together. Any scraps will do. They should be about the size of Christmas cards.

PAINTING

The floor is a good place for the two-year-old painter. The colors won't run and drip as much as they do on an easel or a table. Start off with a big supply of large pieces of paper and a big paint brush, at least three quarters of an inch wide at the bottom. A hardware paintbrush lasts longer and costs less than an artist's paintbrush. For paint and water containers, use a muffin tin or fairly flat, wide plastic bowl.

A child this age does better with just one color. Any kind or color of paper is fine. Try:

> newspaper (a two-year-old will paint right
>   over the print without noticing it)
> large paper bags cut in half
> white butcher's paper (wrappings off your
>   meat packages)
> used gift-wrapping paper
> brown wrapping paper
> shelf paper
> shirt cardboards

Use poster paints. The powder is less expensive and lasts longer, and you need only mix a little at a time. A two-year-old's pictures will consist of a few wavy lines, or dots, or a single blob of color. He tends to discard sheet after sheet with only a line or two on it, so give him the cheapest paper you can find. Don't ask him what his picture is supposed to be; it isn't supposed to be anything. He's learning that he can make his "mark" and that's enough. You may want to save some of his efforts, but he doesn't care a hoot about them. It's the doing that matters.

Fingerpainting (See p. 84)

OTHER HAND PLAY

Puzzles which are simple, big and brightly colored are loved by two-year-olds. You can make them at home quite easily. Try one of these:

Pie Puzzle: Take a piece of thick cardboard, such as the side of a carton, and draw a large circle on it by outlining the bottom of a cooking pot; cut out the circle and then, with a pencil and ruler, divide it into fourths. Color each segment a different color with crayons or poster paint.

Moon Puzzle: Make another large circle and draw a moon three quarters full. Cut the circle into two or three arc-shaped pieces and paint each a different color.

Triangle Puzzle: Make a triangle with four-inch sides. To do this, draw a horizontal line four inches long. At the midpoint of the horizontal line, draw another line perpendicular to the first. Then draw lines four inches long (with a ruler) from each end of the horizontal line to the vertical one. (They should meet.) Cut out the triangle. Then cut the triangle in half along the vertical line. Paint or crayon the two parts.

House or Airplane Puzzles: Cut out of a magazine a large and colorful picture of an airplane, a house, or a boat. Glue it to a piece of cardboard and cut the cardboard to fit it. (Cardboard that comes in shirts is good; so is the backing on large pads of paper.) Then cut the house, boat or airplane into two or three unequal pieces.

Feltboard: Paste a colorful piece of felt (you can buy this in the five-and-ten-cent store) on a piece of heavy cardboard. Cut shapes out of scraps of felt (from old hats), flannel, or velveteen. If you're feeling artistic, you can make animal or people shapes (if you can't draw, trace them) but odd shapes do every bit as well. Show your child how to put the shapes on the felt so that they will stick. This is fine for unsupervised play and creates no mess to clean up.

Cornmeal Sandbox: You can have a small sandpile in your kitchen simply by putting cornmeal, oatmeal or uncooked cereals into a big metal baking pan. If your child puts some meal in his mouth, it won't hurt him. Put the pan on the kitchen table, on newspapers on the floor, or on the back steps. Here are some good things to play with in an oatmeal or cornmeal "sandpile."

funnel	small toy cars and
muffin tin	trucks
sieve	juice cans (with

tablespoon
measuring cup and
   spoons

smooth edges)
empty cottage-cheese **or**
   half-pint cream
   cartons

Spool Stringing: A child of almost three may have enough control of his finger muscles to try spool stringing. Empty wooden spools of thread painted bright colors are as much fun as real beads, and a lot easier. Give him a long string with the ends pointed and stiffened with adhesive or plastic tape. A very long shoelace is ideal. Each spool sliding on the string will represent a lot of hard concentration, so don't push him if he isn't yet ready for this exacting kind of handcraft.

CLIMBING AND CRAWLING

Climbing helps the two-year-old to develop the large muscles of his arms, legs and torso and he is astonishingly sure-footed. If you live in the country or suburbs, you may be able to find an *old wooden ladder* and have someone saw off a section of it, about 3 or 4 rungs (no higher). This can be leaned against a wall or house for climbing indoors or outdoors. You can also make a good bridge by supporting a *large wooden plank* with a couple of *large and sturdy toy building blocks* (just a few inches off the floor or ground). Crawling over this plank bridge helps develop your child's sense of balance.

Planks: Your lumberyard may give away small odds and ends of planks. They will be used endlessly if they are light and small enough for a small child to lug around. Sand them down so that there are no splinters.

GOING PLACES

A two-year-old enjoys an outing most if the whole family goes along. The excursion should be kept short and simple, since his endurance is limited. A walk to feed the pigeons, to hear the peepers in spring, or to visit the local pet shop is enough. If you take him to the zoo, bring his stroller along and make the visit very brief.

READING ALOUD

Between two and three, a child sometimes becomes fascinated by one particular book or record and wants to hear it over and over again. On some days he may listen as long as patience holds out. Be careful not to change a word or skip a line. On other days, he may not be interested at all.

He'll especially enjoy simple stories like *Goodnight Moon* with its many repetitions of words that rhyme.

Books that two-year-olds usually enjoy are listed in the "Children's Books" section. Especially appealing to children this age are *Pat the Bunny, Baby Animals* and *Davy's Days.* They like *Pat the Bunny* because they can do something ("feel Daddy's scratchy face"). They also are fond of books that talk about familiar things. A city child who rides on a bus may like *Big Red Bus;* a child living close to his grandparents might enjoy *Grandfather and I.*

MUSIC AND DANCING

A two-year-old likes music with a definite beat and he "listens" by moving and swaying his whole body. If he has trouble going to sleep at night, you might play him some of the selections from "Music for Falling Asleep" (p. 171), or sing to him yourself. He'll usually want to hear that same song or record over and over again, just like a favorite book.

The song books listed on page 172 are full of children's songs for singing or playing on the guitar or piano. You are still your child's favorite performer.

SIX

Three-, Four- and Five-Year-Olds

A three-year-old is a sociable type. He loves to play or work together with his parents, having them show him just how to do things. He is insatiably curious about the world around him and likes to try his hand at new enterprises.

As he grows older, toward four or five, he begins to prefer to play with his friends, often slightly older children who teach him more new tricks. He's very proud when he succeeds in hammering a nail into a piece of wood or in stringing beads on a shoelace. Be proud, too. These are real accomplishments. If he hasn't developed the necessary manual dexterity or interest yet, don't push him, but praise him for what he *can* do.

Between three and six there are tremendous swings back and forth between striving to be grown-up and wanting to return to the more comfortable life of babyhood. One day a child may want to conquer the whole world (and fully believe that he can!) and the next day he may want to cling and be cuddled. He's torn between his fantasy (and desire) to be big and the terrible reality that he is still very small and needs his parents very much. Support your child's efforts to move forward by helping him master the things which he is capable of doing. Gently distract him from taking on projects that are too much for him to master and will, therefore, make him feel frustrated and defeated. When he's feeling in a clingy or ill mood, let him play in the simpler ways of two-year-olds. The next day, or the next week, he'll start out to conquer again.

A three-year-old's accomplishments are obviously much cruder and more primitive than those of a four- or five-year-old. But that doesn't lessen any of his satisfaction in doing them. Also, a three-year-old will need more help in setting up, beginning, and doing than an older child does. If you enjoy participating and lending a hand, many activities—the painting, clay, pasting ones, especially—can be simplified for a three-year-old.

Some of the activities in this section are dangerous for younger children. So, if you have smaller children as well, be sure they don't get into the older child's playthings.

Some favorite activities carry over from earlier years. These are still popular:

> water (p. 65)—a four- or five-year-old loves whipping a handful of soapflakes into a high foam with an eggbeater.
> cornmeal sandbox (p. 71)
> reserved kitchen drawer (p. 50)
> boards and crates (p. 73)
> feltboard (p. 71)
> spools to string (p. 72)

BUILDING

From three to six, blocks are among the best toys a child can have. Wooden blocks are easily made by sawing 2-inch-by-4-inch lumber into lengths of three, six, twelve, and twenty-four inches. These should be sanded smooth to eliminate splinters. You can also use:

Full Cans and Mix Boxes: You may think of these as things that belong on the shelf, but they can be wonderful toys. In fact, they make better building blocks than any you can buy in the store. Use full cans that aren't too large or heavy. At the first sign of wear, you can rescue the mix boxes!

Empty Milk Cartons: Save gallon, half-gallon, quart, and pint size empty milk cartons and soon you'll have a set of blocks for building forts and doll houses, garages, and even a play house. Milk cartons are lightweight, so the children can have fun crashing them down without making much noise.

Shoe Boxes and Cigar Boxes: If you tape on the lids, they also make fine blocks.

Clothespins: The spring variety make fine construction tools for three-year-olds and up. Just give him a batch and show him how to attach one onto another and you'll be surprised at the constructions that result.

TEARING, RIPPING AND PUNCHING

Before they learn to make things (and after that, too) children love just to rip and tear. Keep a stack of old magazines and newspapers on hand as his "special pile" for "his work." Sit down beside the pile and show him how to tear. Then show him how to poke holes with the handle end of a wooden spoon. He'll have a great time making a snowstorm of newsprint all around him. Afterwards, it can be scooped up in a matter of seconds. Tearing and poking are good ways for a child to learn to use the small muscles of his hands, and also provide a safe outlet for aggressive feelings.

Old Sheets: Let the children tear up an old sheet. They love to rip up cloth! Little boys especially feel strong when they succeed in demolishing a good-sized piece. The pieces make good bandages for make-believe wounds. You can keep a carton or drawer of worn-out linens "just for play." (Don't worry about starting "bad habits." If you give him his special sheet or pillowcase to tear, he won't go around ripping up other things. If you let him vent his energies and strength on this sort of harmless action, he's apt to be less destructive elsewhere.)

Hole Punch: This is a tool which fascinates a child. Just let him punch away on a newspaper. If he uses white waxed paper, save the little punched-out disks. They can be put in a jar full of water and, after you fasten the lid on tightly, he can shake the jar and make a "snowstorm."

Tear a Mural: Give your child a variety of textures of paper (smooth and bumpy, heavy and tissue-thin) and different colors (construction paper and perhaps some patterned paper). Then ask, "Can you tear a *tiny* shape?" "A great big *enormous* shape?" "How about a *wide* shape?" Then let him paste all the interesting ragged shapes on a long piece of paper for a great big, colorful mural. If you have an empty wall, tack the mural on the wall for all to see.

PAINTING, DRAWING AND COLORING

Children delight in making pictures, even if they are just scribbles on a big paper bag or sheet of newspaper. Coloring books are useful at times but children more often prefer to draw their pictures in their own way. He shouldn't be made to feel his picture must look like "something" to grown-ups. To him, it *is* "something" and his imagination is hard at work.

A three-year-old can draw simple shapes like circles or crosses and can also experiment with different strokes. He is beginning to notice the results of his efforts and, in this respect, your praise and encouragement are important. A child puts on paper what he thinks and feels, not what actually exists in the real world. Appreciate his efforts, and let him know that you are accepting him and his unique view of life. If you ask, "What is it?" and he doesn't know, don't press him for an answer. Better not say, "Here, let me help," for he would much rather do it alone.

A three-year-old needs a separate big brush for each paint pot and he can learn to use the right brush for the right color. He can also wash his brushes when he's finished and put them away, if you show him how.

He's happy to paint his pictures sitting either on the floor or at a table.

It is usually not until after his fourth birthday that a child produces paintings which adults can recognize as pictures. By this age he has a pretty clear idea of what he is trying to draw. If some of the proportions or colors strike you as pretty strange, don't let the child know it. If you say, "I like the way you gave that dog those lovely orange ears," he'll be happier. "Whoever heard of a dog with orange ears?" fills a child with doubt and inhibits his next efforts.

It helps if you hang up many of the pictures painted by the child between three and six. Tack them up on walls or hang them by clothespins from a line hung over a stairwell or across the room. They'll be highly decorative.

Paper:

  printers' remnants (often high-quality paper in interesting textures which the printer is glad to give away)

  newsprint paper (largest and cheapest paper available in art stores)

  large paper bags cut in half (all colors; if patterned or printed on, use the other side.)

  white butcher's paper (great for finger painting); save these from your meat purchases or ask a nearby butcher if he can spare a little.

  wallpaper books (use the blank sides for painting and drawing; the patterned sides

may be used for pasting. At certain times
of the year, wallpaper dealers will give you
these books free, because they go out-of-
date.)

brown wrapping paper

shelf paper

shirt cardboards

paper plates

wax paper (This versatile art material is marvelous for tracing, or older children can
scratch pictures on it with a toothpick.
They can also put wax paper over the fun-
nies and rub the surface with a spoon. The
color will come off on the wax paper, making a reverse picture.)

carbon paper (Staple two pieces of paper together with carbon paper in between and
let your child draw with a pencil or crayon. His picture will appear on the second
sheet, too. He'll love this magic.)

PAINT

Flour and Water Finger Paint: Children love to finger-
paint and now and then it's really worth the mess (and
it *will* be a mess). Mix flour and salt with a little water
to make a paste the consistency of thick gravy. Sprinkle in a little food coloring. Cover the children's clothes
with aprons or old shirts and let them paint with
their hands directly on the kitchen table. Put spoonfuls
of the paint on the table, and let them slide their hands
in it. As they work, sprinkle in a little more food coloring to change the color. If you want to save a picture,
press shelf paper over the tabletop art work and the

paint will stick to it. Have a sponge handy to mop up. You can let them finger-paint on the kitchen linoleum floor. The paste isn't tasty but it won't hurt them to put some in their mouths. Food coloring won't stain and you can mop it right off.

Shaving-Soap Finger Paint: Buy a can of shaving soap (nonmentholated) and let him use it on the kitchen table. The smooth texture will delight your child. Some colored powder paint sprinkled here and there will sustain his interest. When soap begins to dry, a few drops of water or more shaving soap can be added. Here the process is more important than the product. When finished, the soap wipes off easily with a dry towel and is less messy to clean up than finger paint. This is good for two-year-olds, too. It won't hurt them to put some in their mouths.

Liquid-Starch Brush Paint:* Liquid starch makes elegant paint. Put a cup of it on the table, give your child a pastry brush, or better still, a hardware paintbrush from your husband's supply, and some dark paper (a cut-up paper bag will do, but dark-colored paper is better). The starch paint will dry on the paper just as poster paint does. If you want to use white paper, add a little food coloring to the liquid starch. If you're out of starch, try:

Soap-Flake Paint: Just mix a little water with soap flakes to make a paste and add food coloring if you wish. This is pretty good paint, but not as effective as starch.

---

* Unsafe for a child who still puts things in his mouth.

If you don't want to bother making paint, get poster paint at the dime store or art-supply shop. Buy the powder, not the liquid; it's cheaper and you can mix a little at a time with water in baby food jars. Two or three different colors are plenty.

Store home-made paints in baby-food jars, which fit conveniently into cardboard soft-drink containers. Six jars of different colors (each with its own brush, preferably) can be easily carried about in this carton with a minimum of spilling. Or put the jars into a muffin tin so they won't tip over.

To dry finished paintings, drape them over a clothes rack or hang them outdoors on a line with clothespins.

PENS, CRAYONS AND CHALK

Ball-Point Pen: Children love to draw with Mommy or Daddy's ball-point pen; they feel very grown-up indeed.

Marking Pencil: A felt-tipped marking pencil is a wonderful drawing toy for a child. Put down some newspaper and give him a big cardboard box to draw on. Keep your child in the same room with you, or he's apt to wander out of sight and begin decorating the furniture and walls! One mother let her children mark hair on their chests to play Tarzan. It took two weeks to wash it out! Get the washable marking pencils. They're easier on mothers.

Crayons, more than any other plaything can be a mother's greatest friend. Like blocks, crayons go on for years but, unlike blocks, they can be tucked into a small bag to be used in doctors' waiting rooms, in the car, or on visits to Granny. For these early ages, be sure to get the large fat crayons that don't break under heavy pressure from little fingers. Four or five different colored crayons are enough.

Chalk: Big fat pieces of soft chalk in vibrant colors encourage free-flowing pictures. The colors mix together easily, making beautiful combinations. (But if your child wants to keep putting one on top of the other until it's all muddy gray, that teaches him about colors too.) Try wetting paper bags and letting him draw on them. The chalk becomes fluorescent.

PRINTING*

Pour a little poster paint or home made paint (pp. 84–85) into a shallow pan and put a few paper towels on the bottom to make a stamping pad. Give your child a few big sheets of white paper (shelf paper is good) or cloth (old sheets are great). Cut a potato in half, or a green pepper, or cucumber, and show him how to rub the vegetable slice over the paint-soaked towels and then print it onto the paper or sheet. (A child may drag the slice back and forth over the paper rather than making one firm imprint. That takes practice and he'll learn in time; meanwhile, he's having just as much fun.)

These things also make fine printing forms:

keys**
hair rollers

* Might be a little too difficult for three-year-olds.

** Watch out for the keys if your child still puts things in his mouth.

sponges
pencils
leaves
half an orange or lemon
a wire whisk
a small wooden spoon

You can use anything which makes an interesting outline and which won't be hurt by the paint. If he's really having fun, you might let him decorate a whole roll of white shelf paper or paper towels.

PASTING

Children love making three-dimensional pictures they can feel. You can use the no-cook flour-and-water paste on page 68. If you use quite a lot of salt, it will crystallize and sparkle when it hardens.

Or you can cook this *homemade "boiled" paste:*

½ cup of flour
add cold water until it is thick as cream
simmer and stir on stove for five minutes
add a few drops of wintergreen to give it a
    pleasant smell
add a few drops of food coloring to make it
    pretty
store in refrigerator in an air-tight jar when
    not in use
    (Boiled paste lasts longer and sticks bet-
    ter than no-cook paste. No harm done if a
    child tastes this paste.)

Collage: is the French name for artistic composition that's pasted together. Give your child a paper bag (cut in half and pressed flat) and let him paste on some:

> crackers
> raisins
> dry puffed cereals
> colored paper scraps
> fluffy cotton
> scraps of colored cloth

Then let him add some lines and color with crayons, magic markers, or chalk. (All these materials are safe for three-year-olds who are still putting things in their mouths; none will stick in the throat.)

Four- and five-year-olds may like to make more elaborate collages. Then they will need Elmer's glue, which is expensive but can be bought more cheaply by the gallon and diluted with water. Pour a little of this diluted Elmer's glue into individual paper cups and let your child dip in with a Q-tip. Collages of eggshells, wood, shells and buttons stay stuck with Elmer's.

Children of four and older can handle blunt-tipped scissors fairly well and most have stopped putting things into their mouths. (If there is any danger of this, don't let them use the materials below.) Here are just a few good collage materials for older children:

> dried-up flowers   leaves
> dry macaroni   dried beans
> large buttons   seeds

small shells   bits of wood
milkweed pods   eggshells

You will think of others.

Paper Chains: Cut a colored magazine picture into one-inch strips. Show your child how to make a circle of one strip, and paste or scotch-tape the ends to each other. Then he can put a second piece through the first circle and glue it together and so on, until he has made a paper chain. These bright chains stretch as long as your child's patience. For Christmas tree decorations, use glossy gift-wrapping paper.

Cellophane Tape and Masking Tape: Children love tearing tape off the roll and sticking it to itself or to anything. If they have trouble handling the sticky stuff, try cutting off a number of small pieces and attaching them to a table edge to be used as needed.

Paper Plates: Children can decorate plates for special holiday parties (with paints or crayons) or make them into funny hats by gluing on decorations and then tying under the chin with a piece of string. A five-year-old may enjoy cutting out numbers from an old calendar and making a clock on a paper plate.

CLAY MODELING

Usually by the time he is four, a child no longer wants just to squeeze and pull and pound a lump of clay. He still enjoys this, but he also wants to *make* something, a real object with a name, which he can save. So he molds streams of snakes, round balls, snowmen, cakes, and dishes. He also likes to paint his creations. By the time he is five, the objects become even more realistic. He often makes separate arms, legs, and heads, and then joins them together to make an animal or a person. Four- and five-year-olds may model human figures with very large breasts and genitals, or with parts broken off or missing. At this age, children are fascinated by the differences between boys and girls. It's natural for them to wonder if perhaps parts of their bodies are detachable or could be cut or broken off. It helps ease such unspoken concerns to translate them into clay. Don't let any exaggerated creations worry you. They provide a good opportunity for you to talk a little about how boys and girls are made.

A good recipe for home made clay:

1 cup of flour, 1 cup of salt, enough water to make a very stiff dough

This home made clay will harden and can be painted. However, it is extremely brittle when dry and breaks easily. If your child finds this upsetting, you will win his gratitude by buying a more durable modeling material. You can get five pounds of pottery clay in art stores for less than a dollar, whereas plasticine is expensive and too difficult for small hands to manage. This pottery clay will last indefinitely if you put it into a large pottery crock with a lid. Make a hole in the middle of the clay in the crock and fill it with water to keep the clay moist. Some pottery clays need to be baked in the oven and others harden into a stone-like finish without heat.

SEWING, BRAIDING AND KNITTING

*Doll Clothes Without Any Sewing:** A little girl can make dresses for her doll by taking a rectangle of cloth, cutting out a head hole (with blunt scissors) and tying it on the doll with a sash. A blouse can be made from a short rectangle; a dress, from a long one; a skirt, from just a length rolled around the doll's middle. Pieces of ribbon add a fashion touch.

*Real Sewing:** The best way to get children started (boys love to sew, too!) is to give them sewing cards.

* May be hard for three-year-olds.

Cut pieces of cardboard in 6-inch squares (covering them with brightly colored paper, if you like), then punch holes about an inch apart around the edges. Show your child how to lace in and out of the holes with a shoelace or a string. (Stiffen the ends of a string by wrapping them with cellophane tape.)

If your child is really interested, give her (or him) a real needle and thread. Cut an 8-inch square piece of loosely knit material which a needle will go through easily. (Have her use a blunt darning or tapestry needle. Standard needles are too difficult for small children and also may cause accidents.)

A four- or five-year-old likes to sew just for the fun of sewing, without wanting to make anything you can recognize. It will become "something" in his or her eyes, however. Some five-year-old girls become passionately interested in sewing and learn to make pouches, crude pot holders, and dolls' capes and skirts (with some guidance and help). They can also sew net into ballet skirts and can be trusted to use electric scissors without hurting themselves (if you stand by).

*Braiding:** Cut heavy wool scraps or old nylons into long, thin pieces. Fasten these to a doorknob and show your child how to braid. This is a fine occupation which can be dropped and taken up again, without having to be put away.

Knitting Needles and String: Sometimes boys and girls who are nearly six can learn to knit with big wooden needles and string (which doesn't separate like yarn). Maybe Grannie will pick up all the dropped stitches for them.

---

* May be hard for three-year-olds.

IDEAS FOR MOTHERS WHO LIKE TO SEW

Cloth Book: Cut four or five pieces of plain colored cloth (the sturdier the better, canvas is dandy) into 12-inch-by-16-inch pieces. Lay them evenly on top of each other and sew a seam down the center to bind them together. Your child can now decorate each page with crayons. When he is finished with his masterpiece, press each page with a warm iron (protect your iron and ironing board cover with two sheets of blotting paper on top of each page and another underneath). The crayon marks melt into the cloth and become permanent.

Rag Doll: On a piece of material, draw the doll's outline, then cut out two identical pieces and sew them together around the edges, leaving a small opening. Turn the doll cover inside out (so the seams are inside) and then stuff it like a pillow with old nylons. After you have filled the body and arms and legs and closed up the opening, sew seams at tops of arms and legs, and you'll have a "jointed" doll. With magic marker, draw a heart on the doll's chest with a secret message—"I love [your daughter's name]".

SORTING

After three, a child loves to sort things. When other friends come to visit, sorting will often keep two or three children busy and happy for twenty minutes or more. It helps teach them to judge size and develops coordination between eyes and hands. An easy way to begin sorting is to let your child help you sort the laundry. Sorting isn't always simple for a three-year-old, so don't be surprised if your child finds it puzzling at first.

*Buttons:** If you have a big collection of all shapes and sizes of buttons, they have many play possibilities. Give each child an empty egg carton, and let him sort them according to size. Or he can drop them into empty salt or oatmeal cylinders. Make slits of different lengths in the lids of several boxes. If you show them how, they can also use buttons to lay out** twisting

* Button games are unsafe for a child who still puts things in his mouth.

** May be hard for three-year-olds.

and intersecting roadways on the rug, but this game takes "billions of buttons."

Cards: Several packs of old playing cards will also amuse a small group of children for quite a while. The younger children can sort the deck into hearts, diamonds, clubs and spades. The older children will want to sort them according to the numbers and pictures which are alike.

Other things to sort (if the children can be trusted not to put them in their mouths) include: lentils, beans, cloves, various kinds of macaroni, shells, coins and old beads.

STRINGING

*Dry Macaroni:** Take some short pieces of macaroni

* Unsafe for any child who still puts things in his mouth.

(the kind with holes all the way through them), and string them like beads to make necklaces and bracelets. The best string for a young child is a shoelace (if you haven't an extra one, take one out of his shoe). If you use string, put cellophane tape around the tip to make it stiff. For gay colors, let your child paint the macaroni with food coloring and dry it before he strings it.

Pipe Cleaners: These are marvelous playthings for almost any age from three to eighty-three. Just twisting them into shapes and attaching them to one another can create an assortment of creatures from elephants to dolls. Regular white pipe cleaners from the tobacco shop are fine, but you can get colorful pipe cleaners of varying thicknesses in hobby shops and some dime stores.

Straws and Pipe Cleaners: Cut the pipe cleaners into two-inch pieces. Show your child how to push a straw onto each end of the pipe cleaner. The pipe cleaner will act as a joint and can be bent in any direction you like. Keep adding more straws (any length you like) and pipe-cleaner joints until he has the "thing" he wants. For variation: Make a hole in a small piece of colored paper and push it on the pipe cleaner before you join it to the straws.

WILD CREATIONS

Most children of four and five, if given an assortment of materials and encouragement, love to make imaginative "creations." Try giving your child some paste or cellophane tape and a motley collection of pine cones, toothpicks, plastic containers, walnut shells, scraps of bright paper and cloth, pieces of cork or potato, old-fashioned clothespins, bits of clay, straws, ribbon and pieces of styrofoam. (You'll think of even better things.) Sometimes, he likes to make "a creation." At other times, he may prefer to make something specific, like a doll out of clothespins, or a boat out of the walnut shells.

*Plastic-Carton Animals:** The plastic cartons used in food stores for berries or cherry tomatoes make good skeletons for animals. A "lion," for instance, can be made by drawing and coloring a lion's face on a stiff piece of paper, cutting it out, and gluing it against one side of the plastic container. Attach pipe cleaners for legs, and yarn for a mane and a tail. It isn't necessary to cover the carton itself with anything. It can also be cut into different shapes with a pair of heavy scissors. Hung from a hanger, it becomes a mobile.

* May be hard for three-year-olds.

Clothespin Dolls: Old-fashioned clothespins make good dolls. Let your child wrap bits of cloth around them for a dress or around the two prongs for pants. A ribbon or string makes a belt. What about hair? (Bits of yarn, clay, paper.) Arms? (Straws, pipe cleaners.) Then show him how to draw the eyes, nose and mouth on the "head" with a crayon or a ball-point pen.

*Walnut-Shell Boats:** Empty walnut shells make fine boats. Use burned matches for masts and hold in place with play dough. Scraps of white cloth or paper can be the sails. These boats are fun to sail in a pan or bathtub. They also add lots to a mobile or stabile.

* Unsafe for any child who still puts things into his mouth.

*Cork or Potato Animals and Towers:** With various size corks and a batch of toothpicks, show your child how to put the toothpicks in a big cork, making legs. Put another in for the neck and add a smaller cork for the head. Then let your child take over and make any wild creature or creation he likes. If corks are hard to come by, use a raw potato, or several of them cut in various sizes.

*Pine-Cone Birds:*** Using a large cone for the body, help your child glue on a smaller one for the head. For the feathers, add wisps of bright paper or real feathers.

*Coat Hanger and Yarn—Stabile and Mobile:*** Take a small empty carton. Turn it upside down and use it as a base for a stabile construction. Push the hook end of a coat hanger through the top of the box. From the inside, bend the hook back and tape it down to make the hanger fairly stable (or make a base for the hook with a large blob of play dough—see page 67). Let the children hang different lengths of yarn from the hanger and fasten all sorts of things to the loose yarn ends. Try:

pine cones**	aluminum foil
plastic spoons or forks	cookie cutters
pieces of colored paper	shells**

---

* Unsafe for any child who still puts things into his mouth.
** May be hard for three-year-olds.

MAKE-BELIEVE

Children from three to six love to make-believe that they are almost anything from tigers to airplanes. But most especially, they like to pretend that they are grown-ups—truck drivers, train conductors, firemen, office workers and Mommy and Daddy.

So when you're cleaning out bureau drawers or closets, save some of your husband's old clothing as well as your own. Your small son will also enjoy pretending to shave with an old razor (with blade removed), shaving brush and soap. If his father carries a lunchbox or briefcase to work, he will have fun swaggering around the house with his own.

Boys like dressing up in parts of uniforms, too—police badges, armed services insignia, fireman's hats—as well as cowboy boots and hat. So do girls.

Boys as well as girls like to dress up in Mommy's skirts. This is perfectly natural at this age. If your son smears lipstick on his mouth, don't give it a second thought—except to save your favorite lipstick. This doesn't mean he's going to be a "sissy."

Make-believe doesn't begin or end with dressing up. It is very strong in children of this age and shows itself in everything from daydreaming to playing with paints and clay. Puppets are another fine form of make-believe and "acting things out"; so are storybooks. Trying to sort out the "real" from the "pretend" world is an important task of the three-, four-, and five-year-old. He's working at it all the time.

Kings, Queens and Cowboys: For dress-up, here are

some bits of old clothing both boys and girls will treasure:

Women's

dresses	aprons	ruffled
shoes	pocketbooks	petticoats
skirts	artificial	veils
any uniform	flowers	ribbons
blouses	jewelry	hats
coats	scarves	

Men's

shoes	work aprons	armed services
shirts	work pants	insignia
pants	mufflers	badges
hats	wallets	caps
		any uniform: police, doctor, mailman, military

Keep them all together in a big box for the moment someone asks, "What do we do now, Mommy?"

OTHER GOOD "DRESS-UP" MATERIALS

Aluminum Foil: If the occasion is a very special one and you are willing to use this expensive stuff, you can make your child very happy. For a girl, crunch a circle of foil into a crown for a princess or a fairy. Cover a spoon or stick with it to make a wand or scepter. For a boy, cover a hat with foil, then tear off two large sheets of foil, and put one against his chest and the other against his back, like a sandwich board. Crunch them together at the shoulders, tape them together securely, and he becomes a knight in shining armor! You can cover the top of a large soap box to make a shield.

Large Paper Bags: These make wonderful masks, with holes cut out for the eyes. If he wants a fancy mask, a child can color the outside, paste on yarn for hair, paper for ears, etc.

Castles, Caves and Airplanes: A chair may be just a chair to you, with or without a smudge of chocolate on the cushion. But to a little child, chairs, tables, and beds can become boats or trains or a whole house. It doesn't take more than a small suggestion from you to jog their imaginations.

A bed can be a boat for a trip. If the children get off the bed, remind them that they are in the water and had better swim back to their boat.

A row of chairs can be a train or an airplane. Give the children some food (apples or cookies) for the trip.

A spare table near the chairs can be the diner. Send them off with a few books for reading on the train or plane.

A *card table or kitchen table* with or without a bedspread or blanket over it, can be a house or a cave.

A *small trash container* of heavy-gauge metal makes a fine horse to sit astride.

Empty toilet-paper or paper-towel rolls make realistic horns, megaphones, and telescopes, especially if you wind colored cellophane tape around them. Give your child one, with the suggestion that he play, "band man," "sailor at sea," or a "spaceman" looking at other planets.

Large cardboard cartons, three or four in a row, can be a train. The "conductor" can use an egg carton to collect the "fares" and give out "tickets" made from torn-up pieces of paper. The "vendor" can sell the passengers real magazines and peanut-butter sandwiches. Small bags of cookies and raisins can be carried by the passengers for the "trip."

A *paper plate* can be a steering wheel. Then the row of cartons can become a car or boat. For variety: make a loop for a child's hand in a length of clothesline and tie the other end to a carton. The children can then take turns pulling each other in the box, and get rid of excess energy while having fun.

Empty food cans and boxes make a fine play store. Save a big collection of old ones for a rainy day "store."

Rinse them out but be sure to leave the labels on. Tear up bits of aluminum foil for paper money or cut green paper into "bills" with pinking shears, and use buttons for coins. An egg carton makes an excellent cashbox. The children will have a fine time pretending they're real storekeepers. Some especially good cans and boxes to save in your closet or basement:

cookie	cracker	teabag
salt	juice	coffee
fruits	soup	vegetables
baking powder	cocoa	soap powder

A sock can be pulled over the end of a broomstick for the head of a hobby horse. Stuff the sock with old pieces of materials and tie it tight at the "neck" around the broomstick. If you like—and your child doesn't put things in his mouth—add buttons for eyes and a piece of red material for the tongue.

PUPPETS

Small paper bags can become hand puppets, if you help your child draw faces on them. A white bag can be a ghost; a shiny ice-cream bag could be a knight. If you make a little hole for the mouth, the child can poke a finger through it and make a "tongue." Two fingers may be ears.

Old socks and old mittens also make good hand puppets. A child can slip his hand into the toe of his sock and make the puppet "talk" by moving his thumb up and down against his four other fingers. If you feel

like it, sew two buttons on the toe section for eyes and another for the nose; a slip of colored material may be sewn on for the mouth.

Potato and Apple Puppets: With a corer or knife, make a hole in an apple or potato large enough for a child's finger. Stick on (with a small piece of toothpick) two slices of stuffed olive for eyes, or carve off pieces of the apple or potato skin for features, or use whole cloves. A handkerchief wrapped around the child's hand becomes the body, and he wiggles his finger to make the puppet move.

A Hand Can Be a Puppet: With a washable marker, draw two eyes, a nose and mouth in the creases of your child's palm. By moving his fingers, a child can create all kinds of amusing expressions; if two children's hands are decorated, they then have four puppet characters to talk back and forth.

*Doll Houses:** Store-bought doll houses seldom give a small child enough room to play with her doll family. It's really easy to make a home made doll house, and it will be a lot better than one you buy. A doll house can be open either at the top or on one side, in which case each room is like a little stage. You can make either kind from several sturdy corrugated cartons. (Liquor stores have the most durable kind, but the grocery-store cartons for heavy canned goods will do.)

With a small paring knife, cut out doors and windows on the sides. A one-story roofless house makes it very easy to reach inside, but if your child wants a roof, make a removable one with a large, flat piece of heavy cardboard, or two or three of these cartons can be piled on top of each other to make a house of several stories. This is best done with the open-side variety. If the box is wide enough and long enough, divide it with a cardboard partition, so that there are two rooms.

Your child can paint the interior walls of the house with bright poster paint or paste on leftover wallpaper, or cloth. Contact paper makes wonderful doll-house wallpaper. Small scraps of heavy material make good rugs.

Wooden cigar boxes, round cheese containers, and wooden matchboxes make sturdy tables and beds. Glue on match sticks or small dowel rods for legs. Little cardboard gift boxes can also be transformed into bathtubs, beds, and tables. They don't have to look like the real thing. A piece of cloth will transform a box into a "bed"; a bit of soap or sponge will make it a tub.

---

* May be hard for three-year-olds.

A doll family can be made from pipe cleaners and clay or from round-headed clothespins (pp. 80, 98). However, the store-bought variety of tiny dolls of flexible rubber or jointed plastic are really more satisfactory because they can sit down. They are also easier to dress and undress.

Play Houses: Huge corrugated shipping cartons for stoves, refrigerators and other large appliances usually make marvelous playhouses. Some refrigerator companies even include directions about how to convert their packing boxes into houses, fire stations or forts. Although you or your neighbors may not be about to buy a stove or refrigerator, you may still be able to get a carton from the appliance buyer at one of your local stores. Sometimes they are happy to give away the boxes of their floor models. Another possibility is to look in the yellow pages under "paper-corrugated" and make inquiries of the companies listed there.

For a house, cut out a door and a window. Your child can paint it with poster paint and a big brush and then decorate and furnish it. Scraps of old cloth make good curtains. (Help him stick them up with wide masking tape.) An old cushion or two will make a good chair or bed, and a few pots and pans give him a kitchen. If "the house" is going to be used outdoors, it will last a little longer if you paint it and drag it under cover at night. The simplest way is to spray it with a spray-paint can. Do this when your child is napping, because otherwise he'll want to help. Spray-paint and small children don't mix.

At about the age of three, children enter a period of comparative quiet and not so many members of the family get punched, kicked, or scratched. But another

The Fall Guy—A Special Doll

idea—a very good idea—has dawned: hitting some*thing* is almost as good as hitting some*one*, and it doesn't get you into so much trouble. Punching or throwing a teddy bear seems safer than attacking a younger sister or a mother. Sometimes young children spontaneously pick on one of their own animals or dolls to use as the "fall guy" for their rages and frustrations. They hit him, lecture him, and kick him around. Sometimes giving the child a special doll made for this purpose can be a great help to him.

Why are these rages necessary? Why can't children

be taught not to get angry and not to hit anything? Learning new skills—how to throw a ball, how to use a spoon, how to sit at the table—is a difficult job and, oftentimes, frustrating. One of a child's main reasons for learning is that his parents want him to. He wants to please his parents, but it's a hard job. He has to learn to control his hand muscles, his feet muscles, his eyes, his ears, his bowels. Frustration and anger are inevitable if a child is developing. Unlike grown-ups, who can hit a tennis ball or go bowling or spill out their feelings to a sympathetic friend, a young child has very few outlets for his frustrations. But he can learn to take his anger out on things rather than people, and that's a big step forward. Help him find ways to do this.

Many mothers and nursery school teachers have found "fall guy" dolls work wonderfully well. Sometimes it's a good idea to make enough dolls to represent your whole family—mother, father, the baby (that's a particularly important one if there is a new baby), and the older sister or brother.

Here's an easy way to make a *Fall Guy*. From a piece of canvas, cut out a doll's head and sew it together after stuffing it with old nylons. Embroider features on the face with colored thread. The hair can be yarn sewed on to the canvas with a big needle. Be sure it is sewed securely so that it can be yanked a lot. These dolls don't need any bodies. Simply sew onto the canvas neck a woman's blouse, or man's shirt, or an old baby shirt. Choose the clothing that fits your family.

Against this "fall guy," children can, without causing harm, get feelings out where they belong—in the open. Bottled-up feelings can cause trouble later. You'll be surprised at how well these dolls can work.

COOKING AND CLEANING HOUSE

They Want to Help Mommy: Many jobs around the house are fun for children. They can be happy and busy while you work and they love to feel they are working by your side. A child of five wants very much to be useful and "help Mommy."

A three-year-old may not be much real help to you but he is often a very eager worker. Don't discourage him. Choose something simple that doesn't require precision or careful attention and something which you don't mind having done somewhat sloppily. He'll soon learn to master his trade.

Washing dishes is a real pleasure for most children, once in a while. Let the younger ones begin with unbreakable pots and pans, plastic dishes, or tableware. Five-year-olds can usually handle breakable things without damaging them.

Setting the Table: A child of three can learn to distinguish right from left by setting the table with place mats, napkins, and tableware. Older children can add the glassware.

Washing woodwork, refrigerator, stove, chairs, and counters is satsifying work. Give the child a dishpan half-full of soapy water. Show him how to squeeze out the sponge, and then let him go to work. This will actually produce some good results, and many areas will be spic and span after his persistent rubbing.

Dusting and Vacuuming Are Fun: While you dust, let your child push the vacuum cleaner. When you need to use the vacuum, he can polish the furniture with the dustcloth. Three-year-olds can begin to learn to take turns.

Sorting the Silverware: A child over four can straighten your tableware drawer, matching spoons, knives, and forks in small batches.

Washing Vegetables: Give your child the vegetable brush and let him scrub the potatoes, carrots or beets.

Preparing Vegetables: All children like husking corn, tearing up lettuce, shelling peas, breaking up beans. Give your child a dull table knife and let him chop up a potato. You can cook it or throw it away (it will please him more if you cook it).

COOKING WITHOUT HEAT*

Icing: If you're baking cup cakes, make a basic white icing:

¼ cup	soft butter
3 cups	confectioners' sugar
3–4 tbs	milk
1 tsp	vanilla

Give each child a dab of icing in a paper cup and let him add his own food coloring. He can then spread the colored icing on a cup cake, decorating with sprinkles of chocolate "jimmies," or raisins, chopped nuts, or tiny bits of jam or jelly. (If you're baking a cake, the

---

* May be hard for three-year-olds.

children can dribble leftover icing over plain crackers and add "jimmies" or raisins.)

*Instant Pudding:** Children enjoy opening packages of Jello and instant pudding (no cooking required) and adding the cold milk or water you have measured for them. (You add the boiling water to the Jello.) To make the pouring and stirring easier for them, let them stand on chairs next to the kitchen table. Vanilla instant pudding becomes pink, green, yellow or blue with a few drops of food coloring. Let each child color his own pudding in a small paper cup and then decorate it with bits of marshmallow, striped peppermint candy, nuts, raisins, or squirts of canned whipped cream.

Lemon and Orangeade: You will find that children love to squeeze fresh oranges and lemons on the hand juicer; and can add the sugar and water for a delicious cooling drink. With some help, they can fill an ice tray with real fruit juices and freeze them into cubes.

Dinner Salads: While you're fixing dinner, the children can make fruit "faces" on halves of pears or peaches. Let them decorate with cherries, raisins, slices of apple or carrot curls. Pear halves make fine bunnies if you show them how to stick in sliced almonds for ears and make cottontails of cottage cheese.

*Stove Cooking:** A five-year-old considers it a great honor to be allowed to turn the breakfast pancakes. If you stand by to supervise, he can scramble eggs, make

* May be hard for three-year-olds.

toast, and cook hot dogs. He will also enjoy slapping and patting his own hamburger, and then cooking it. Better not cook anything else on the stove while you are watching over his cooking. Pick a time to let him cook when you don't have to keep an eye on any younger children.

Cooky Rolls: ° These are sold in the grocery store in the frozen-food section. The rolls can be cut up easily with a dull table knife. The cookies will be oddly shaped, but the children will learn to cut, to count, to line up on the cookie sheet, and to use a cooking "timer." Most of all, they'll love watching you eat something *they* have made.

GAMES

Bowling Alley: ° Save ten half-gallon milk cartons. Take one regular-sized, unopened soup can, and you have a bowling alley. The children can roll the can on its side across the kitchen floor and knock over the carton tenpins. (Maybe you'd better put a pillow behind the cartons so the can doesn't crack the wall.)

Newspaper War: Let the children crumple newspaper into ammunition balls and arrange forts of cardboard boxes for a good battle. No one gets hurt and lots of "fight" gets played out.

Broomstick and Hat Game: Tie a broomstick to the back of a chair, put an old hat on top and see if the children can knock it off with a dry sponge or bean bag.

° May be hard for three-year-olds.

Circus Toss: Cut a good-sized hole in an old sheet and drape it on a chair or table. Let the children try to throw a dry sponge through the hole. For a party, paint a big face on the sheet, using the hole for the mouth.

Toss Game: Use big buttons or playing cards and an old hat (or shoe box). Let your children see how many cards or buttons they can get into the hat.

Puzzles: You can keep one child or a group entertained for quite a while with magazine-picture puzzles. Choose one large colored magazine illustration for each child and paste it on a piece of cardboard. Then cut it up into four or five pieces for the child to put together. When he can do it easily, exchange the puzzles. Finally, make the puzzles harder to assemble by cutting them all up into very small pieces.

PLAYING WITH MUSIC

Singing and Dancing: A three-year-old can sing snatches of songs and will enjoy jumping around the room in time to music. By the time he is four, he usually recognizes melodies and is able to sing whole songs. Because the four-year-old is so fascinated with make-believe and is willing to take turns in group play, this is the fine age to introduce him to those wonderful old-time singing games such as "Ring Around the Rosey," "Here We Go Looby Loo," "Farmer in the Dell," and "Here We Go Round the Mulberry Bush." (Words and music can be found in the songbooks listed on page 172.)

If you can play the piano even a little, your child from three to six will be an appreciative audience. At five, many children can pick out simple tunes with one finger—if you show them how. They can also begin to produce crude rhythms in time to music.

Dancing becomes important to five-year-olds although they really are not ready yet for dancing classes of any kind. With a little suggestion from you ("You're an Indian," or "You're a willow tree in the wind" or "You're an elephant"), a five-year-old can crouch, bend, weave, tiptoe and work out fairly elaborate dances in time to music. Children like best to dance in bare feet. A dance session in loose pajamas and bare feet just before bedtime is good fun and helps relax a child for sleep.

Wearing a hat or holding something in his hand often does away with self-consciousness and frees a child's movements and imagination as he dances. Give him some silk scarves, colored tissue (or crepe) paper, or a large feather or leaf. Any hat will do fine (see goofy hats, page 120) or try a paper mask (see page 104).

THE SOUND OF MUSIC

Almost all children from eight months to six years (and seven, eight, nine, or ten) have a marvelous time with these home-made musical instruments:

Pot Lids: Two flat lids make a *cymbal.*

Flour Shaker: Put some dry macaroni in the shaker, tape the top on securely and you have a razzle-dazzle.

Large Empty Cans: Easy to hold and bang. Be sure there are no rough edges. Leave the labels on or take them off. The effect is the same.

Wooden Spoon: Fine for striking cans and lids.

Cardboard Cylinders From Paper-Towel Rolls: After you've used up the paper, make the cylinders into fifes and bean rattles. For a fife, punch five small holes in a row down the top of the empty cylinder. Then cover one end with waxed paper and fasten it securely with cellophane tape. When your child hums a tune into the tube, the sound is amplified. By covering some of the holes on the top with his fingers, he can produce different notes.

Empty salt boxes filled with a handful of rice or pebbles make good rattles or *maracas.* (Tape the opening in the lid securely so the rice or pebbles won't spill out.)

Empty oatmeal boxes become drums and tambourines. Either tape the lid onto the carton with adhesive tape and let the child thump and shake the whole thing, or give him just the lid for a tambourine.

Empty paint cans with both ends removed make even better drums. Cut two circles, large enough to cover the ends of the can, from an old rubber inner-tube, and punch holes around the edges of the rubber circle with a paper punch or scissors. Cover the ends with the rubber circles and then lace them tightly to one another by drawing a string or shoelace through the holes and back and forth along the side of the can. Plastic or leather shoelaces are best.

Hair combs covered with toilet tissue become harmonicas. They have a nice brassy sound. Show the child how to hold the tissue-covered comb against his mouth and sing or hum with his mouth slightly open. It tickles, too.

A *shoe box* with the cover removed and eight or ten rubber bands of different sizes stretched around it makes a *harp* or a *guitar* to be plucked.

Building Blocks: Tack or glue sandpaper to one side of two wooden blocks. When they are rubbed together in time to music, the sandpaper produces a shuffling dance-band beat.

Brown paper bags (or any other color) make goofy hats for the band players. Roll back the edges into different shapes for the brims. You can lead the parade into the back yard to attract more recruits.

Records: When choosing music records for the three- to six-year-old, don't overlook grown-up records, such as folksongs, classical music, jazz and rock 'n' roll (see record list pages 167–172). A small child won't listen quietly to Mozart (unless he is a born musician) but it makes pleasant background music for finger-painting, and for helping a restless child fall asleep.

Whatever special kinds of music you like—Basin Street jazz, African folksongs, opera, or the blues—will probably please your child, too. The important thing is sharing it.

The same is true of the "activity" records. The first time he hears one, he'll love it if you go through the motions with him.

Story records are good for quiet times when you are busy and can't read to him. They are also helpful for children who are convalescing and must stay quiet. But the impersonality of a record can never replace the intimacy of your reading to him.

PLANTS AND ANIMALS

Even in a small city apartment, a child under six can
learn about nature. Scoop up a spider, some ants or
worms in a glass jar. (If you're too squeamish, get
somebody else to do it!) Punch a few holes in the lid
to allow the creatures to breathe, and add a handful
or two of dirt, some grass or leaves. Let your child
watch the ants and worms make tunnels and the spider
spin a web. A magnifying glass makes the watching
even more absorbing. After a few days, take the insects
to a patch of grass and let them go.

PLANTS

How a Plant Drinks: Fill an old glass with water and
some red food coloring. Then cut off the bottom of a
stalk of celery or a carrot and let your child put it in
the colored water. In several hours, let him cut open
the vegetables with a blunt knife. The celery will be
peppermint-striped; the carrot inside will be bright
red. This "surprise" shows how a plant drinks water.

What Else a Plant Needs: Let your child wet a bath
sponge and sprinkle grass or bird seed over it. Put the
seeded sponge on a plate and cover it with a clear glass
dish. Leave it on a sunny window ledge and let him
water it daily. When the blades of grass appear, remove the glass cover. After a while, put an opaque
bowl over the grass. In a few days, see what happens.
What does a plant need besides water?

Funny Potato Face: Scoop out some of the pulp from
the top of a large potato and put some moist cotton

into the little hollow you have made. Then slice off the bottom of the potato so that it will stand up, and put it in a small dish of water. Let your child sprinkle grass or bird seed over the moistened cotton. In a few days, if he waters it faithfully, the potato face will sprout a wonderful head of green hair. He can then make eyes, nose, and mouth with garlic cloves.

Roots Are Fun: Take a few kernels of corn or dried lima beans and soak them overnight. Then show a child how to moisten a piece of cotton and put it into the bottom of a glass and add a few kernels of corn. Soon he can see the root tendrils spreading out through the glass, and then the stems growing up through the cotton toward the air and light. (Be sure he keeps the cotton moist.)

Trees From Seeds: Grapefruit, orange, and lemon seeds can be soaked overnight and planted in some rich potting soil. If kept well-watered in a sunny spot, they eventually will sprout dark glossy leaves and grow into small trees.

Onion Flowers: Put three toothpicks into a large onion and then suspend it over a small glass of water so that only the bottom of the onion is in the water. Put it on a sunny windowsill. It will send up graceful green leaves and eventually produce a flower.

Eggshell Gardens: When you are cooking something which requires a lot of eggs, save the shells for a child's garden. Let your child fill each half shell (nested in an egg carton) with dirt and plant a large seed such as a zinnia or dwarf marigold, or a dried pea or lima

bean (after it has been soaked in water overnight). Keep the garden moist. Not all the seeds will sprout but at least half of them should. When an inch and a half tall, they can be transplanted to little pots and later planted in the garden.

Sweet Potato Vine: Set the narrow end of a sweet potato in a glass of water and put it into a dimly lighted place, such as a closet. In ten days it will begin to sprout and you can move it to a sunny spot. If you keep replacing the water in the glass, the potato will soon become covered with graceful shoots and leaves and produce a very pretty vine for the kitchen window. Let your child help you with the daily watering.

Pineapple: Show your child how to slice off the top two inches of a fresh pineapple and let it dry on a saucer for ten days. Then you both can plant it in a small pot of damp sandy soil. Keep it moist and in a month, after it starts sprouting roots, transplant it to a large pot filled with sandy potting soil. This makes a dramatic and different-looking house plant, and who knows, it may even produce a pineapple.

Avocado Pit: This seed requires a long waiting period (often as long as six or seven weeks) but once it starts to grow, the changes happen quickly. Be sure you pick a ripe pit to start with.

First wash the avocado pit with warm water, then insert several toothpicks to suspend one third of it in a full glass of water. Put it in a warm place in dim light for four to seven weeks. Your child can add more water as needed. Tell him that the pit should split and start sending out a stem and roots. He'll be thrilled to tell you when this finally happens. Then you can move it to the light.

When the stem is about five inches high, you should plant the pit in dirt in a big flower pot (at least nine inches in diameter). If you keep it in a sunny spot and water it about twice a week, it will soon be as tall as your child. This experiment is best for older children. It's hard for younger ones to wait so long. Even older ones forget about watering in the long first sprouting period. It's more fun after it's sprouted.

ANIMALS

Most children even at a very early age like animals. But they can't be expected to take care of them until they are six or seven. Unless you have older children, the care and feeding of cats, goldfish, guppies, whatever pet you get, will fall into your hands. Also, very young children have no concept of their own strength and the harm it can do. Many young children have inadvertently hurt or killed a baby kitten, or salamander by squeezing it too hard. Until he is five or six, it is really too much to expect a child to gauge the difference between squeezing and holding very gently. So you will need to be with a child when he's playing with a baby pet and keep showing him how to hold it.

On the other hand, there is nothing like taking care of a living thing. Watching a kitten or gerbil or a goldfish play and grow is a wonderful experience in fun and learning. A five-year-old can begin to observe and question in a real way. What does an iguana eat? How does a gerbil make his house? Does the chuckwalla like one part of the cage better than the other? Is a kangaroo rat shy? What do newborn kittens look like? For very young children, it's the watching—not the handling—that is the greatest part of the fun.

Home made Bird Feeder: If you live in the country or in the suburbs, your child will be able to watch many birds come and go. Even two-year-olds like to look out the window and find a bird at the feeder. Older children will notice the different sizes of the birds and will enjoy watching for the birds they see in bird books. But, according to the Audubon Society, city children in large metropolitan areas have little chance to be visited by any birds other than pigeons, starlings, and English sparrows.

A four-year-old can make a bird feeder from an empty half-gallon milk carton. With blunt scissors, help him cut out two windows about an inch from the bottom of the carton. Make the windows about two or three inches wide and about one inch high. (If they are higher, the seed will blow out onto the ground.)

It's difficult to paint a waxed carton but your child can decorate or cover it with contact paper. Heavy aluminum foil makes a nice cover, too. (Regular paper, of course, will get soaked in the rain.)

Run a piece of string, cord, wire, or clothesline through the peak of the carton so that you can hang the new feeder on a nearby branch or porch rafter. Put a handful of bird seed or a piece of suet in the bottom.

Here are some pets which are both easy to look after and particularly suited to small children.

Cats are the traditional standby. They are fun to watch at play, especially when they are kittens, and they can be very affectionate—when they want to be, of course.

Not requiring much exercise, they are easy to keep in apartments. When you go away, you often can leave your cat with friends or neighbors without fear of complications. Most cats can take a lot from children, but there are some which, when pushed to the limit (pulled by the tail, for instance), will scratch. This attack can be frightening to a small child. (Be sure the child's tetanus inoculations are up-to-date.)

Dogs are really a family affair—for Mother, Father and all the children. Everyone in the family should agree on the need of having one. Dogs need people for company and play—they respond to people more than most other pets do. It isn't long before a puppy is a member of the family, but he will need a lot of petting, patting

and training. A family really shouldn't take on a dog unless they can give time and attention to him.

Certain breeds are less high-strung than others and

can tolerate the teasing and playing of the very young. If you are considering getting a dog, ask a veterinarian what kind he thinks is best for your children and your particular living arrangements. Some dogs get enough exercise on a leash in the city; others really need to roam the wide-open spaces. Most dog breeders say that, if you are going to have a dog around small children, you should get the dog as a puppy. He should grow up around the children and be familiar with their play from the start.

Goldfish, turtles, and guppies all require little care. The main problem is keeping them alive. Be sure you oversee the feeding. Many a goldfish has perished because of eager overfeeding. Young children under six have little time sense and don't realize that the fish's last meal was just a few hours ago or that a fish won't eat as much as they do! Keep the fish food on a shelf and bring it down once a day. Show your child how much (a little) to sprinkle into the fishbowl. Turtles of the five-and-ten-cent-store variety can't take too much handling so they're best for watching. They like to crawl up and over smooth obstacles. A flat rock is a good thing to put in a turtle's home, which can be any width bowl three inches deep. Make sure the rock sticks out of the water so the turtle can rest on it.

Turtle water sometimes carries bacteria which can cause an infection in children known as salmonella. After handling turtles, children should wash their hands and of course, should not be allowed to drink turtle water. Nor should any other pets.

Feed your turtles every two or three days. In addition to turtle food, which is dead flies, they like all kinds of worms, earthworms, mealworms, raw hamburg, raw chicken, raw liver, any kind of raw fish. Some have been known to nibble at small bits of tomato, banana, strawberries, or even spinach. Let them eat as much as they want to. Usually a turtle's appetite is satisfied with a tablespoon of food. Once a week, mix Turtle Hard-Shell drops with their food. These help keep the turtle's shell hard, a sign of good health, and can usually be purchased at pet stores for less than one dollar.

An anthill is a fascinating project for a five- to six-year-old. He can watch what goes on and keep track of how the ant colony changes over several months. An anthill can be bought inexpensively at most dime stores and comes in a tight flat container—you needn't worry about your house.

Small desert animals are ideal in many ways. They are clean, odorless, easy to keep and care for, gentle to handle and can be left untended over weekends and short holidays. You can make a desert terrarium from a large wooden crate, an old leaky 20-gallon fishtank,

or a large plastic breadbox (the kind you can see through). Allow one square foot per animal. Any less will crowd them. Make a screen cover that overlaps the side. For their own sake, be sure the animals can't jump or crawl out and get lost or eaten by other pets. (They won't do any harm to anyone else.) Fill the bottom with dirt and sand and plant a small cactus here and there. Add a rock, a dirt-filled flower pot and a strong twig to climb on. Twice a week throw away left over bits of food. Every six weeks, change the dirt and sand. Here are some good desert animals:

Kangaroo rats look gentle, are gentle and don't resemble rats at all. They fit easily in the palm of your hand. They like to burrow in a small dirt-filled flower pot. Keep the pot in the terrarium cage with a secure cover. Kangaroo rats can leap three feet into the air and, although they'll do no harm if they escape and probably won't get hurt, they are hard to find. Because they are nocturnal animals, they tend to make burrows in the dirt or stay hidden in their flower pot all day—just when a child wants to watch them. One way to get around this is to tack red cellophane to the sides of the terrarium cage. The kangaroo rat is fooled, thinks it's almost nighttime and becomes more active. Feeding kangaroo rats is no problem. Give them three teaspoons of bird seed and a leaf of lettuce or fruit every day. Once in a while throw in a few pieces of dog chow.

If you also have a dog or cat, watch to see if he is jealous of the kangaroo rat or other pets. Make sure the terrarium lid is secure. He might make off with one.

Don't be hesitant about taking the kangaroo rat out

of the terrarium and letting your child stroke him.
Grasp his tail firmly near the base and lift the animal
from the cage and into your cupped hand. Carry out
this maneuver over the open cage so that, if you drop
him, he'll fall on something soft. Let his feet come in
touch with the surface of your cupped hand as soon
as possible because he won't like to feel himself dan-
gling in midair. Hold him in your hand with the tail
between your fingers. When a child becomes used to
petting and feeling the animal, let him hold the kangaroo rat himself. Be sure your youngster doesn't hold
him too tight.

Iguanas are a kind of lizard, 12 to 15 inches long, and
live happily in a desert terrarium, too. They are most
active when their body temperature is over 90°. Put
a low lamp (a metal goose-neck lamp is ideal) on top
of the mesh terrarium cover. A 100-watt bulb will do.
If the temperature goes below 55°F., the iguana will
become sluggish, so, if it's cool, leave the terrarium
light on.

Iguanas like to climb. Don't be shy about putting
things in an iguana's cage. He will crawl up a twig and
rest on a rock. During the day, the iguana will leave
his burrow in the sandy bottom to laze under the lamp.
Now and then he'll search for food. Two ounces of lettuce (not more than a small leaf) is his daily portion
and, occasionally, you can give him a small piece of
apple or pear.

A *chuckwalla* is a lizard, too, and he can live in the
same terrarium with an iguana or a kangaroo rat, as
long as each has enough room to roam about. From
snout to tail tip he is about 12 inches long. A favorite

chuckwalla food is dandelion flowers but chuckwallas, like people, seem to have individual preferences. Try bits of succulent fruits until you find the one your particular pet likes most: melon, grapes, banana, lettuce. But never give him more than a total of two ounces a day.

Iguanas and chuckwallas benefit from frequent handling. If they inflate with air, don't be surprised. They do that when they are frightened and want to scare another desert animal. The shyness decreases with familiarity. You should be the one to take them out of the terrarium. Grasp an iguana or chuckwalla on the body between the front and back feet. (The iguana may lose his tail if you grasp him by it. Luckily, over the course of several months, he'll grow a new one.) You'll be surprised how fast they are, so keep a firm grasp on them until they quiet down. Your child can hold him and stroke his rough, scaly skin to soothe him. Both iguanas and chuckwallas like the warmth of a hand.

Gerbils have become very popular in the last few years. They are beguiling little furry animals that fit neatly into your hand. They can live in a glass terrarium, a wooden box, a discarded bird cage or even an old bookcase covered in the front with wire mesh. They must, however, live by themselves, because, although they make marvelous pets for young children, they are bad neighbors for lizards and kangaroo rats. They thrive on bird seed (especially sunflower, squash, and pumpkin seeds), cabbage leaves, pieces of pear or melon, dog chow. Each day they should eat three tablespoons of dry seeds and one ounce (a bit) of lettuce or fruit. Gerbils like to gnaw at plastic, cardboard, wire—anything. This doesn't mean that they're trying to escape, or that they're starved. They just need to gnaw.

The wonderful thing about gerbils is their curiosity. They are always bustling around their cage. Put a topless glass jar inside the cage and watch them. Or try an empty toilet-paper roll, some old socks, bells, paper, blocks, a toy ladder—anything you or your child think the gerbil would have fun with. Don't worry about cleaning the gerbil's cage. Once every two or three weeks is plenty. They make only a few droppings of highly concentrated urine each day and eat their own droppings. In fact, if the cage is cleaned too often, it can lead to a vitamin deficiency.

Gerbils, like identical twins, look exactly alike. If you have more than one, mark each one's forehead or ear with food coloring or a dab from a felt-tipped pen so that the children can tell them apart. Older children can see how long it takes for a gerbil to change its coat.

Gerbils are fun to watch and fine for older children (five and six) to hold. They like to crawl up arms and hide in pockets. You should be the one to take them from their cage. As with the kangaroo rat, lift them out by the base of the tail and drop them gently into your cupped hand.

Gerbils almost never bite or scratch hard. For this reason they are more popular than hamsters or guinea pigs. But if a gerbil becomes overexcited or frightened, he may bite the finger he usually nibbles with affection. If the skin is broken, be sure to check with your doctor about tetanus.

If you have a male and a female gerbil, watch for a family. Babies are usually born in fours or fives, but sometimes a mother will give birth to as many as eight or nine. The babies are small, about the size of a paper clip. Adult gerbils seem to manage during the birth beautifully by themselves. The father gerbil stays in the cage during the birth and may wash the babies while the mother gerbil keeps them warm and feeds them. You might wonder if you should do something to help the mother and father gerbils. Actually they are best left to themselves during birth and for the next two or three days. You can help by seeing that the family is left alone, for at this time sharp noises distract them. Just make sure that there is plenty of paper or bits of rag in the cage so they can make a nest if they want to.

Baby gerbils are very delicate at birth and rarely does a whole litter survive. Explain this to your child as soon as you see the newborn litter (you may not know in advance that the mother is pregnant). Be sure to reassure him that this almost never happens to human babies. Your child may be very sad to find out that even if he is quiet, tiptoes near the gerbil cage and leaves the mother alone, still some or all of the babies may die. But the prospect of death is no reason not to get a male and a female gerbil, or any pet for that matter. The death of a pet is sad but can be a valuable experience for a child, even a very young child of two or three. Because it may be a child's first experience with death, explain to him the real facts in simple terms and let him express his feelings openly and ask any questions—no matter how silly they may seem to you. The death of a baby gerbil or a goldfish may not be hard for you, but it may be quite an event in your child's life and one he needs help in understanding.

Be sure that you treat the death of a pet—any pet, a dog, a cat, goldfish, guppies, baby gerbils—with the respect due to a living being. Don't flush the dead guppie down the toilet or throw the turtle out with the garbage. Children may worry that they, too, will be flushed away like the fishes or thrown in the garbage. Help your child bury the dead pet (in a cardboard box) in the backyard or a nearby park. Even if your child is very young, bury the dead pet while he is there to watch you do it. This may seem like quite an undertaking on a busy day but it is particularly important for a child to make this connection with realities of life and death.

WORKING WITH TOOLS

Around three or four, children yearn to make something real with the real tools that father uses—or with the real needles that mother uses. Both boys and girls usually love to work with wood because it produces something so substantial. How early they begin depends upon how much supervision is available. Many nursery schools let children start hammering and sawing at the age of three. But in a busy household, when you can't be close at hand every moment, it's better to wait until four or five. In any case, you or your husband will have to lend a lot of help at the beginning, and thereafter keep a watchful eye on their efforts.

For materials, you will need:

a small crosscut saw
small hammer
big-headed three-, four- or six-penny nails

sandpaper

Elmer's glue (use in a small paper cup with a Q-tip)

lumber scraps, available free at your local lumber yard (pick small pieces without jagged edges or knots, with the grain running *lengthwise,* as in wood flooring, to avoid having the nail split the wood)

scraps of styrofoam, available from your local drugstore

A Good Workbench: Nail two wooden planks (at least two inches thick) to a low table or two heavy wooden crates. This will be more satisfactory than a wobbly child's workbench bought at a store. A child learning to saw and hammer needs lots of elbow room and the table should be low enough for him to work comfortably, (about two feet from the floor).

A good first construction is a styrofoam "thing" with a bunch of lumber scraps, glue, pieces of colored wire, styrofoam, and other bits of beautiful junk. A child will enjoy making something of his own which stays together. Show him how to push large nails into the styrofoam with his hand, and attach pieces of wire, paperclips, etc., to the nailheads. After he's through constructing, he may like to paint his creation with poster paints.

Hammering Nails: If you're lucky enough to have a yard big enough to hold an old tree stump or railroad tie, these are ideal for hammering practice. It helps his aim if the child holds the hammer by the middle of the handle. Show him how to hold the nail and ask him to keep his eye on it. He may hit his fingers a few times, but he's not strong enough to hurt himself. He'll soon get the hang of it and enjoy it immensely. (This is good activity for girls, too.) Inside, let him work on the floor with a long (to keep it stable) and thick (two to three inches) piece of soft pine.

Sawing: Soft pine is the easiest wood to saw, if it is free of knots. You will probably have to make the first few strokes to get a child started. Then you had better stand by until he's finished to see that he doesn't hurt himself.

GIFTS YOUNG CHILDREN CAN MAKE

(If the sawing is too difficult, an adult can help.)

Blocks: Show him how to saw up different lengths of 2-by-4-inch lumber. Then let him sandpaper, wax (paste, floor wax), or paint each block.

Plant or Pot Stands: Have him try cutting thin pieces of wood (such as plywood) into 6-inch squares. Draw the squares for him before he starts. When he's finished, he can sand and wax (paste, floor wax) them.

Bookends: Have him nail together two pieces of wood (at least two inches thick, about six inches long, and four inches wide). This makes one bookend. For a second, have him repeat the process. Then he can paint them with poster paint.

REAL HARDWARE TO PLAY WITH

Magnet: A child loves the magic of picking up pins, nails, or paper clips with a magnet.

*Padlock and Key:** A big one is best. The key is easier to fit in the lock.

Magnifying glass: to examine snowflakes, insects, flowers.

Discarded alarm clock is fascinating to take apart.

An old folding ruler: to measure with. This makes a wonderful toy but a young child can break it fairly easily. Don't give him a good one you care about.

* Watch out for the key if your child still puts things in his mouth.

OUTDOORS

Your backyard may end up looking like a junkyard, but both boys and girls from three to six learn valuable skills and have many good times with old inner tubes, rubber tires (which make good swings but are also fun to roll), empty metal paint cans, packing cases and barrels. Save old heavy plastic shower curtains and tablecloths for tepees.

Constructions: Four-year-olds enjoy constructing bridges and towers and then climbing to the "very top." For this they will need (in addition to the beautiful junk mentioned above) some long planks for ramps and some sturdy wooden boxes, such as those used for carrying milk bottles. (Perhaps your local dairy will give you some they are about to discard.) After a boy has pulled himself up to the pinnacle of his structure, the ground may suddenly look pretty far away to him. If he calls for help, give him a hand but do it casually. Sometimes it's humiliating to a four-year-old to be rescued by his mother.

By the time your child is five, he will climb rope ladders, knotted ropes, and trees. You may shudder to watch him, but don't worry. He's surprisingly sure-footed. This age loves swings and stilts, too. Sandbox, mud, and water are still intriguing.

*Painting:** A hardware paintbrush and a can of water can turn your child into a painter. Let him brush with water the house, his tricycle, the fence, and even your

* Unsafe for a child who still puts things in his mouth or who may yield to temptation to taste the paint.

car. It will seem effective to him because the object
he paints will change color when it's wet. A five-year-
old may not be so satisfied with "water" painting; he
may want to do "the real job—like Daddy." If you have
the time to supervise and an old shirt you don't mind
getting covered with paint, let him try painting something with real oil paint. He won't be very accurate
but it will encourage him to take on real-life jobs, and
by the time he's twelve you may have a really good
handy-man around the house.

Gardening: Save a small patch of the yard for a garden.
If you have no sunny spot out back, a tomato or squash
plant will grow well in a tub on the front stoop. Choose
seeds which are large enough for a child to handle
easily and are hardy growers. Zinnias, marigolds, ca-
lendula, aster and morning glory are good choices
among flowers; corn, string beans, lima beans, and peas
and tomatoes make a good vegetable garden. Any
child under six will need help with watering and weed-
ing, but when it comes to picking the vegetables, he
can enjoy this all by himself. Let him also husk the corn
and break the string beans for cooking.

OUTING WITH GROWN-UPS

Visiting places where something big is going on gives
a boy or girl many ideas for imaginative play later on.
It's hard to play "Daddy at work" when most children
today haven't any notion what Daddy does all day.
Even exploring his own house with you can give a
child a sense of discovering his own family history.

A Journey in the House: If you can spare thirty min-

utes, take your child by the hand and lead him on a tour of discovery. Talk about the pictures on the wall, a cherished vase, the begonia plant or Grandfather's chair. Explain what they mean to you and encourage him to ask questions. Poring over old family photographs or pulling everything out of an ancient trunk in the attic can be fascinating to a child. Sorting silverware together, taking special pains to compare the different patterns help him become more aware of beauty everywhere. A stroll through the back yard looking for birds' nests or worms, or looking carefully at every tree and flower is fun if Mother is along, too. A child will appreciate a half an hour of your complete attention and conversation far more than the most expensive toy or gadget you could buy for him. You are giving him something infinitely more precious to him—your own thoughts and feelings.

A Trip to See Daddy at Work: This is an adventure which brings a young child closer to his father. Afterwards you can help make a "Daddy's Work Book," by tearing out magazine pictures and pasting them on pieces of cardboard. (Make these into a scrapbook by tying them together with shoelaces.)

Start the book with breakfast and follow Daddy through the day at the wheel of his truck, or in the factory, classroom, or office, until he drives or takes the train home. On each page, write down his comments about each picture, based upon his own personal observations. In this way an important experience is translated into something a child can hold in his hands and relive.

Other ideas for outings are used successfully by many nursery school teachers every year. But they

work even better with one child or smaller groups because they can be more spontaneous and can allow more time and space for wandering around.

A Nature Hike: If you live in the country or can get there easily, try a trip just to feel out the details of nature. Children often love looking at things closely and feeling new objects in detail. Don't undertake this trip if the idea doesn't give you any pleasure. You'll be impatient, and your child won't have much fun either. But, if you're the kind who likes to be out in the fields anyway, try looking at them from a child's point of view. He likes to see and feel the little parts of things, such as leaves and berries. And see how birds build their nests or cows chew the grass.

Unless you are an expert botanist and know exactly what is poisonous, don't let your child put any grasses or berries in his mouth. Teach him that it is important not to taste wild plants because he can never be sure they aren't poisonous unless he grows up to be an expert.

You don't need to wait for sunshine. A gusty day with high-flying clouds or a foggy, drippy day all have their special sights, and smells. Take along a big magnifying glass. Here are just a few of the *things that are fun to smell* (watch out for poison ivy):

honeysuckle   seaweed

skunk cabbage   clover
sassafras bark   wild blackberries
wild strawberries   wintergreen
dandelion leaves

What do they look like under the magnifying glass?

For Touching and Looking:

different kinds of tree bark,
    from rough pine to smooth beech
leaves
all kinds of grasses

milkweed pods
moss and mushrooms (no tasting)
sea shells

What do they look like under the magnifying glass?

For Watching and Listening: What are these animals and insects saying to each other? How do they live? Where are their houses? What do they eat?

birds	peepers and frogs in a pond
squirrels	dogs
cows	crickets and katydids
horses	

Other Places to Visit: The visits of three- and four-year-olds are of the "peek behind the counter" variety. They like to visit small local shops. If you have a friendly butcher or grocer, ask him if he'll let your child go behind the counter and step inside the big freezer to see the meat hanging. Construction sites—big or small—are also an endless source of wonder. Children love to watch the big cranes, the bulldozers, the cement mixers, the wreckers, and the big trucks, and to see the workers in their hard-top hats. Other special places are:

The Post Office: Early morning is the busiest and most interesting time to visit. Write a small note to your child and put it into an addressed envelope. Let him buy a stamp at the counter, put it on the letter and mail it in the proper slot. Then, if you can, go behind the front counter to see the workers sorting mail and canceling stamps. Perhaps the mailmen will show your child where they put the mail for your street. When the postman comes to your house the next day, your child will have his lettter delivered to him. It's a kind of magic.

The Fire Station: Better telephone first to make sure the engine and firemen are there. If they're not too busy, they are usually glad to let your children try on a fire hat, watch a fireman slide down the pole, and inspect the engine thoroughly. How does the fire alarm work? Where do the different firemen stand on the truck, and what does each of them do at the fire?

The Florist: On a cold winter's day when the earth is barren and gray, visiting a large greenhouse lifts everyone's spirits. A five-year-old with a passion for detail will like studying the flowers through a magnifying glass. A workroom where bouquets, baskets of flowers, and corsages are assembled makes good "looking" and smelling, too. Why are the flowers growing inside the greenhouse and not outdoors?

The Food Factory: Any food factory is interesting whether it's ice cream, soup, or spaghetti popping out of pipes and vats. Canning and bottling factories are fun too. In large plants, there are often guided tours and samples to taste. Call up first and ask about it.

The Printing Press or Newspaper Press: This usually requires telephoning ahead to discover when the presses are going to be busiest and if you may visit. At big-city newspapers, a newsprint expert will usually be on hand to explain things. Children, especially, are fascinated by the trimming process. Be sure to bring home a supply of paper remnants for home art work. When the children are a little older, they may want to produce a newspaper of their own.

The Police Station: Call the desk sergeant on duty and ask if you can visit with the children. He may show them the inside of a police car, demonstrate the two-way radio, and give them a short safety speech. If a few petty criminals or drunks get pulled into the station, that's educational, too. Are there a couple of jail cells in the back?

The Farm: A city child will especially enjoy visiting a large farm with a variety of animals, but he will want to explore everything thoroughly. This means watching the cows being milked and the pigs fed, climbing up the ladder to the hayloft, collecting eggs in the hen

coop, going down into the springhouse to hear the frogs. Boys will want to climb up on the tractors, too.

The Pet Shop: This is good for an hour's visit if there are birds, guinea pigs, rabbits, and tropical fish. Pet-store owners are usually most hospitable to children, if they don't bang on the fish tanks. Your problem will be getting out of the store without buying a parrot, monkey, or pet alligator.

The Library: A children's story hour is a good way to introduce your child to a library. As soon as he shows any interest in books, see if your library has children's cards and let him choose his own reading matter (with some help from you). On a summer vacation, away from home, rainy days will be a lot pleasanter if you invest in a summer membership in the local library.

Other Good Places to Visit:

> a tall tower with a view
> museums with special children's exhibits
> airports
> a busy harbor
> a zoo
> a railroad station
> subway ride (if this is a novelty for him)
> ferry ride
> buildings and roads under construction
> cement being poured
> road being tarred
> big cranes in operation
> power shovel
> bricks being laid
> telephone wires being repaired

READING ALOUD

A mother of nine once said that by the time her ninth child was born, she knew all the bedtime-story books backwards and forwards. You may, too. Even with one child.

At anytime of day or night, reading is perhaps the best way to soothe a weary or frightened child. Or entertain a restless one. By holding him on your lap or sitting close beside him, a mother and child are brought close together by touch as well as talk, and, at the same time, the story provides entertainment for both. The bedtime story is the time-hallowed transition between the active day and sleep. Four- and five-year-olds are more prone to night fears than other ages and a reassuring book can make a great difference.

When you read to a child, encourage him to interrupt you and talk about whatever he likes. The stories and pictures may remind him of himself or his playmates or the dog that scared him or something else that happened in his day. He may want to talk it over with you. Often a book will free a child to talk about some things that are bothering him that he doesn't quite dare to bring up directly. It's easier for him to say "You see Curious George is scared" than it is for him to say "I am scared." This leaves you a good opening to say "Are you scared? I get scared, too, sometimes. What are you frightened about?" Many small worries and wild and woolly fantasies that upset small children are often laid to rest this way.

If you can, keep a child's books in his own room where he can browse through them when he feels like it. Even a two-year-old has feelings about the books he has. Library books borrowed over and over again can become as familiar as bought ones.

Three-year-olds often enjoy stories about animals. They don't have to be familiar ones—elephants and crocodiles hold as much interest for them as dogs or kittens. But the stories should still be kept rather short.

By the time he's four, a child is a much better listener. He likes funny exaggerations, but he is also a realist who is very much interested in the *how* and *why*. Pictures should still be clear and the text brief.

The five-year-old can follow action stories with good plots. He also likes realism and fantasy (if not too frightening), prose and poetry. He not only wants to be read to, but he wants to tell his own stories about something he has done or seen or may retell a story in his own way. If you have time, let him dictate a story, and write it down on large sheets of paper—a few words per sheet. Then suggest he make his own pictures for it. He'll be proud of his "very own book."

There's a controversy over fairy tales. Many childcare experts feel that it's better to wait until a child is seven and is able to distinguish better between fantasy and the real world before reading most of them. *Hansel and Gretel, Little Red Riding Hood,* and even the *Three Little Pigs* can be scary with their cruel stepmothers and devouring wolves, and there are many other stories which are just as entertaining for children this age (see pages 158–165 for some suggestions).

BATH TIME

After an active day, there's nothing like a bath to soothe an excited child or comfort a tired one. Particularly in a household of many children, bath time can be a valuable period of quiet and private play. If your child enjoys the bath, try not to rush him through it, even though you may have other things to do. A child should not be left unwatched in the bathroom until he is at least six years old. Younger children can't be expected to be agile or alert enough to keep their heads above water if they slip and fall—or if they go to sleep while bathing. This means you'll have to be in the bathroom with him or in the very next room where you can see or hear clearly that he is all right. Plan your day so you can do something—tidy up, read or sew—*very near-by.*

In the bathtub, children really prefer to play by themselves. They like a private time to talk to themselves, sing, splash, soap themselves and daydream. The conversations you hear are a child's way of practicing the complicated language he has heard all day; it's like the dialogue he may have with himself before he falls asleep at night.

Five-year-olds also like to experiment with water. In addition to regular bath toys, let your child try out a few household odds and ends so long as they are safe. This is a chance for him to begin to discover what water does to things and how things behave in water.

What happens to paper in the bathtub? To cellophane? To tinfoil?

What happens if you crunch up the tinfoil into a small ball? Will it float?

Why does the water go through the sieve?

Do soap bubbles last longer on cellophane or tinfoil?

Will plastic boats float upside down?

What happens to an ice cube in the bath? In a soap dish?

Does your hand look different at the bottom of the tub?

Children love to play with the plastic liquid soap containers that are shaped like animals. They will fill them and empty them, then fill them and empty them again. Which holds more water? Which lets the water out fastest? Which one can be filled fastest?

Sponges and sponge animals are fun in the tub, too. Is a wet sponge bigger than a dry one?

Put a few blocks into the tub. It won't hurt them. Do they all float? Even the big ones? What about plastic blocks? What things don't float?

A bubble bath makes the tub easier for you to clean and adds to a child's fun. He can blow the bubbles down to his toes and try to blow them into the air. How long do they last? Does a block float in bubbly water, too?

Appendix

Children's Books

Everyone has his own favorite children's books. This particular list was put together by a group of librarians and nursery school teachers and includes the books they find their children like best. When you pick out a book for your child, look for one that interests you as well; after all, it's you who must do most of the reading.

Because books are expensive to buy, we have included—with a few exceptions—only those books which are available in libraries. We have made an exception of *Pat the Bunny* and *Tickle the Pig*, because they are "touch-and-do" books and fun for very young children. At the end, we've made a special small list of good books that cost $1.00 or less. These aren't usually available in libraries either.

FOR THE TWO- AND THREE-YEAR-OLDS

Margaret Wise Brown,
> *Goodnight Moon*
>> A little rabbit says goodnight to all the familiar objects in the room.   (Harper & Row, $2.95)
>
> *A Child's Goodnight Book*
>> A marvelous bedtime story.   (Harper & Row, $3.50)
>
> *The (City) Noisy Book*
>> The little dog Muffin could not see when his eyes were bandaged, but he could hear.   (Harper & Row, $2.95)
>
> *The Little Fur Family*
>> A little fur child goes out to play in the woods, but when darkness comes runs home and is given a warm supper and tucked into bed by his mother and father. An excellent bedtime book.
>>
>>   (Harper & Row, $2.75)

The Quiet Noisy Book
Muffin, the little dog, is awakened by a quiet sound. Was it an ant crawling? A bee wondering? Butter melting?
(Harper & Row, $2.95)

The Country Noisy Book
The reader can experience sound effects with Muffin in the country. (Harper & Row, $2.95)

Baby Animals
The text and colorful illustrations help acquaint children with some animals. (Golden Press, $1.50)

Marguerite de Angeli,
Book of Nursery and Mother Goose Rhymes
Verses to learn by heart. This edition makes a fine present.
(Doubleday, $5.95)

Marjorie Flack,
Angus and the Cat
The scottie makes a new friend. (Doubleday, $1.50)

Angus and the Ducks
Angus, the scottie, gives in to his curiosity and explores behind a hedge. (Doubleday, $2.25)

Ask Mr. Bear
Thanks to Mr. Bear, Danny finally found the very best birthday gift ever for his mother—a great big bear hug.
(Macmillan, $2.95)

Mary M. Green,
Everybody Has a House and Everybody Eats
Tells how every animal has his own special house and how every animal and child has his own special way of eating. (Scott, $2.75)

Ethel and Leonard Kessler,
The Big Red Bus
The big red bus goes to the end of the line and back the other way. (Doubleday, $2.95)

Ruth Krauss,
The Bundle Book
A game is played by a mother and her little girl, who is hiding under the covers. (Harper & Row, $3.25)

Dorothy Kunhardt,
Tickle the Pig°
A touch book in which one can scratch the giraffe, tickle the pig, wiggle the octopus and other fun things. (Golden Press, $1.95)

Pat the Bunny°
Paul and Judy do fun things like patting the bunny and then invite the child to do the same. (Golden Press, $1.95)

° Touch-and-do books not generally found in the library.

Lois Lenski,

Cowboy Small

Children find great satisfaction in following the doings of Mr. Small on the Bar S Ranch.   (Henry Z. Walck, $2.25)

The Little Auto   (Henry Z. Walck, $2.25)

The Little Farm   (Henry Z. Walck, $2.25)

The Little Train   (Henry Z. Walck, $2.25)

More humor and action in the life of Mr. Small.

Davy's Day

A day of a child's life.   (Henry Z. Walck, $1.95)

Surprise for Davy

A birthday in the life of a child.   (Henry Z. Walck, $1.95)

I Like Winter   (Henry Z. Walck, $1.95)

Now It's Fall   (Henry Z. Walck, $1.95)

Spring Is Here   (Henry Z. Walck, $1.95)

Sweet little books of winter, fall and spring activities.

Thomas Matthiesen,

ABC

An alphabet book.   (Platt and Munk, $2.50)

Things to See

Beautiful color photographs of familiar things.

(Platt and Munk, $2.50)

Grace Skaar,

Nothing But Cats and All About Dogs

A good reading practice book for beginning readers, in one volume, with large, poster-like pictures of all varieties of cats and dogs.   (Scott, $3.50)

Robbie Trent,

The First Christmas

This story of Jesus' birth told briefly in rhythm and richly colored pictures is just right for very small children.

(Harper & Row, $2.50)

FOR THE THREE- AND YOUNG FOUR-YEAR-OLDS

Dorothy Aldis,

All Together—A Child's Treasury of Verse

A selection of fine poems which have been especially loved through the years.   (Putnam, $3.75)

The Runaway Bunny

A little rabbit threatens to run away from his mother, who tells him all the ways she will bring him back. Good reassurance of parental love.   (Harper & Row, $2.95)

Helen Buckley,
  Grandfather and I
    Only Grandfather has time to spend with a little boy. What a
    happy time it is for them both.   (Lothrop, Lee & Shepard, $2.95)
  Grandmother and I
    The warm, happy relationship between a little girl and her grand-
    mother, whose lap is a most comforting place.
                                      (Lothrop, Lee, & Shepard, $2.95)

Marie Hall Ets,
  Gilberto and the Wind
    A little Mexican boy finds that the wind makes a fascinating
    playmate.   (Viking Press, $3.00)
  Play with Me
    Illustrated in soft tones, this book tells of a little girl who learns to
    play with the meadow animals.   (Viking Press, $2.75)
  In The Forest
    A small boy's idea of his walk.   (Viking Press, $2.25)
  Just Me
    A little boy imagines he can match the antics of his animal friends.
                                           (Viking Press, $2.50)

Barbara Geismer and Antoinette Suter,
  Very Young Verses
    An engaging collection of poetry. A favorite of nursery school
    teachers.   (Houghton Mifflin, $3.00)

Ethel and Leonard Kessler,
  Do Baby Bears Sit in Chairs?
    What animals do and don't do. A lovely rhyming story.
                                           (Doubleday, $2.50)

Phyllis Krasilovsky
  The Very Little Girl
    A little girl grows enough to have a surprise.
                                           (Doubleday, $2.50)
  The Very Little Boy
    A small boy gets bigger page by page   (Doubleday, $2.50)

John Langstaff and Feodor Rojankovsky,
  Over in the Meadow
    A fresh and lovely picture book based on an old animal counting
    song.   (Harcourt, Brace, and World, $3.50)

Watt Piper,
  The Little Engine That Could
    The perennial favorite about a little blue engine who "thought
    he could" pull the stalled train over the mountain.
                                           (Platt & Munk, $1.50)

Miriam Schlein,
> *Shapes*
>> An introduction to the observation of the shapes around us.
>>> (Scott, $2.75)

Charles G. Shaw,
> *It Looked like Spilt Milk*
>> A picture book in blue and white showing some of the many shapes a cloud may take to the imaginative young mind.
>>> (Harper & Row, $2.75)

Irma E. Webber,
> *Up Above and Down Below*
>> How plants grow with their leaves above the ground, their roots below.   (Scott, $2.50)

Garth Williams,
> *The Rabbits' Wedding*
>> A wholesome story about a black rabbit and a white rabbit who fall in love.   (Harper & Row, $2.50)

H. R. Wing,
> *What Is Big*
>> A *Little Owl* Arithmetic Book designed to make quantitative comparisons meaningful to children of this age group.
>>> (Holt, Rinehart, & Winston, $1.95)

Ethel Wright,
> *Saturday Walk*
>> Exploring the community with Daddy.   (Scott, $2.50)

Gene Zion,
> *Harry the Dirty Dog*
>> How Harry's need to be recognized has to contend with his hatred of baths.   (Harper & Row, $3.25)
> *No Roses for Harry*
>> Harry, embarrassed by Grandma's birthday present, has lots of adventures trying to get rid of it.   (Harper & Row, $3.25)

FOR THE FOUR- AND FIVE-YEAR-OLDS

Helen Bannerman,
> *Little Black Sambo*
>> When Little Black Sambo goes for a walk in the jungle all dressed up in his best clothes, he outsmarts the tigers who want to make a tasty meal out of him. Perhaps a bit scary in the beginning.
>>> (Platt & Munk, $1.35)

Lorraine and Jerrold Beim,
  Two Is a Team

  A distinguished picture book about the friendship of two little
  boys, one Negro and one white. (Better for 5- to 6-year-olds.)
                              (Harcourt, Brace, and World, $2.75)

Bemelmans,
  Madeline

  The first tale about Miss Clavel and her 12 French students.
  Illustrated with gay, full-color paintings.   (Viking Press, $3.50)

Elsa Beskow,
  Pelle's New Suit

  The reader sees how the wool of a lamb is first carded, then spun
  into yarn, woven into cloth, and finally tailored into a new suit for
  Pelle, a little Swedish boy.   (Harper & Row, $3.25)

Margaret Wise Brown,
  SHHhhh . . . BANG!

  Here is a whole town in which all the people whisper. A fine
  reading-aloud book.   (Harper & Row, $2.95)

Myra Berry Brown,
  First Night Away from Home

  Amusing story of what Stevie considers are the absolute necessi-
  ties for spending the night with a friend.

                              (Franklin Watts $2.95)

Virginia Lee Burton,
  The Little House

  The classic story of a little house which is crowded out by the city
  growing around it.   (Houghton Mifflin, $3.50)

  Mike Mulligan and His Steamshovel

  Mike's pet steamshovel wins a bet but digs itself into a problem
  that requires a surprising solution.   (Houghton Mifflin, $3.25)

  Katy and the Big Snow

  All about Katy, the Crawler Tractor, who saves the day when the
  city is visited by a blizzard.   (Houghton Mifflin, $3.50)

William Cole,
  I Went to the Animal Fair

  A gay collection of animal verses, complete with illustrations.

                              (World, $2.75)

Lucille Corcos,
  Joel Gets a Haircut

  A 5-year-old goes to the barber.   (Abelard-Schuman, $2.75)

P. D. Eastman,
  Are You My Mother?

  A tale about a baby bird who is trying to find his mother. A
  delightful and humorous story.   (Random House, $1.95)

Encyclopedia Brittanica,
   The Monarch Butterfly
      An interesting book about the life cycle of the monarch butterfly.
                              (Encyclopedia Brittanica Press, $1.56)

Aileen Fisher,
   Where Does Everyone Go?
      In rhythmic verse the reader discovers where many woodland
      animals go when the weather turns cold in the fall. Colorful
      illustrations.   (Thomas Y. Crowell, $3.50)

Marjorie Flack,
   Story about Ping
      Year after year children love to hear the adventures of this little
      duck on the Yangtze River in China.   (Viking Press, $2.00)
   Tim Tadpole and the Great Bullfrog
      The tale of an ambitious tadpole.   (Doubleday, $2.50)

Wanda Gag,
   Millions of Cats
      A classic story of an old man's search for a kitten and the millions
      of cats that follow him home.   (Coward-McCann, $2.50)

Hardie Gramatky,
   Little Toot
      The story of a beloved little tugboat who finally learns to master
      his frivolity.   (Putnam, $3.50)

Mary M. Green,
   Is It Hard? Is It Easy?
      Things that are hard for one person may be easy for another.
                                          (Scott, $3.25)

The Brothers Grimm,
   The Shoemaker and the Elves
      The warm and satisfying tale of human goodness and kindness
      rewarded, with lively and subtle illustrations. (Schrbner's, $3.25)

Helen Kay,
   One-Mitten Lewis
      Lewis lost things more than any other little boy in town—espe-
      cially mittens.   (Lothrop, Lee, & Shepard, $2.95)

Ethel and Leonard Kessler,
   The Day Daddy Stayed Home
      Because of a blizzard, Daddy stays home and plays with the chil-
      dren. Wonderful fun.   (Doubleday, $2.00)

Dorothy Kunhardt,
   Nurse Nancy
      Boy and girl play doctor and nurse. Book comes with bandaids.
                                          (Golden Press, $2.25)

Lois Lenski,

Let's Play House

A natural for little girls. Mother's household activities are an exciting game for this age group.　　　　(Henry Z. Walck, $2.25)

Lionni,

Inch by Inch

An inchworm who maneuvers into a precarious position with a community of birds runs afowl of a hungry nightingale. Children love the canny inchworm's solution.　　　　(Obolensky, $3.95)

Edna Miller,

Mousekin's Golden House

A gentle story of a small whitefoot mouse who finds a home in a discarded jack-o-lantern.　　　　(Prentice-Hall, $3.95)

A. A. Milne,

Winnie-the-Pooh

Absurd and delightful adventures of Pooh, Christopher Robin, Piglet, Kanga and Baby Roo.　　　　(Dutton, $3.50)

Robert McCloskey,

Make Way for Ducklings

A story about the ducks and the Swanboats in Boston's Public Garden.　　　　(Viking Press, $3.50)

Blueberries for Sal

Sal and her mother, Babby Bear and Bear Mother, pick blueberries on the same hill in Maine. Adventures follow.

(Viking Press, $3.25)

Phyllis McGinley,

The Horse Who Lived Upstairs

Joey, the city horse, lives in a stable which is reached by an elevator. He longs for the country, and one day, he gets his wish.

(J. B. Lippincott, $3.95)

Emmy Payne,

Katy-No-Pocket

To find a place for son, Freddy, is the problem of Katy, the pocketless kangaroo.　　　　(Houghton Mifflin, $3.50)

Beatrix Potter,

The Tale of Peter Rabbit

The nursery classic about an adventuresome rabbit and his escapade in Mr. McGregor's garden.　　　　(Warne, $1.80)

The Tale of Flopsy Bunnies

Peter Rabbit and his cousin, Benjamin Bunny, have more exciting adventures when they try to rescue "The Flopsy Bunnies"—Benjamin's troublesome offspring.　　　　(Warne, $1.25)

The Tale of Jemima Puddle Duck

Jemima was a foolish duck who thought she could hatch her own eggs but failed to reckon with the wiles of the courteous "foxy-whiskered gentleman."   (Warne, $1.25)

Helen Puner,
   Daddies, What They Do All Day
      Pictures and rhymed text are answers to the questions small children ask about what their daddies do.   (Lothrop, Lee, $2.95)

H. A. and Margret Rey,
   Curious George   (Houghton Mifflin, $3.25)
   Curious George Flies a Kite   (Houghton Mifflin, $2.95)
   Curious George Takes a Job   (Houghton Mifflin, $3.25)
   Curious George Gets a Medal   (Houghton Mifflin, $3.25)
   Curious George Goes to the Hospital   (Houghton Mifflin, $3.25)
   Curious George Learns the Alphabet   (Houghton Mifflin, $3.25)
   Curious George Rides a Bike   (Houghton Mifflin, $3.25)

H. and N. Schneider,
   How Big Is Big?
      More complicated version of *What Is Big?* The relation of a boy to things larger and smaller than himself in our universe from stars to atoms.   (Scott, $1.95)

Dr. Seuss,
   The Cat in The Hat
      When Mother and Father leave home for the day, the Cat with a very big hat entertains the children.   (Random House, $1.95)
   The Cat in the Hat Comes Back
      The Cat returns to amuse the children while Mother is away.
                                          (Random House, $1.95)

Esphyr Slobodkina,
   Caps for Sale
      The peddler who loses his caps to a tree full of monkeys and gets them all back again is a never-failing favorite.   (Scott, $2.75)

Vivian L. Thompson,
   The Horse That Liked Sandwiches
      Mario (the horse) gets himself and Tony, his owner, into trouble by eating other people's sandwiches. Finally on a children's picnic he gets all the sandwiches he can eat.   (Putnam, $2.50)

Alvin Tresselt,
   White Snow, Bright Snow
      This picture book captures the silent fall and whiteness of snow.
                                          (Lothrop, Lee, $2.95)

   Rain Drop Splash
      Many raindrops made a puddle into a pond, a pond into a lake, which overflowed into a river and ran down to the sea.
                                          (Lothrop, Lee, $2.95)

   Hide and Seek Fog
      Only the children find the fog a happy challenge in a seaside village.   (Lothrop, Lee, $3.50)

Tasha Tudor,
> *Around the Year*
>> Each month of the year is described in simple verse.
>> (Henry Z. Walck, $3.25)

Tomi Ungerer,
> *Emile*
>> Emile the octopus saves Captain Samofar, becomes a lifeguard, captures smugglers and becomes a hero.   (Harper & Row, $3.25)
> *Crictor*
>> A funny book about an elderly French spinster who has a pet constrictor.   (Harper & Row, $3.25)

Bernard Waber,
> *The House on East 88th Street*
>> The captivating story of Lyle, the crocodile who won his way into the Primm family's hearts.   (Houghton Mifflin, $3.25)

I. and G. Wilde,
> *I Want to Be a Farmer·*   (Children's Press, $2.50)
> *I Want to Be a Truckdriver*
>> What farmers and truck drivers do.   (Children's Press, $2.50)

Books for a Dollar or Less

FOR THE TWO- AND THREE-YEAR-OLDS

H. A. Margret Rey,
> *Where's My Baby?*   (Houghton Mifflin, $1.00)
> *Feed the Animals*   (Houghton Mifflin, $1.00)
> *Anybody at Home*   (Houghton Mifflin, $1.00)
> *See the Circus*   (Houghton Mifflin, $1.00)

FOR THE THREE- AND YOUNG FOUR-YEAR-OLDS

Margaret Wise Brown,
> *The Color Kittens*
>> Two little kittens, Brush and Hush, mix colors and make others. Tells a child which colors when put together will make others.
>> (Golden Press, $.29)
> *Golden Egg Book*
>> A little bunny and an egg become very attached to each other, and when the egg hatches, the duck and bunny become even better friends.   (Golden Press, $1.00)

Five Little Firemen

The job of each fireman is explained when the five go to a fire.

(Golden Press, $.29)

The Poky Little Puppy

Four puppies dig under the fence and go out into the world. Poky puppy gets all the rewards until the hole is plugged up and he is too slow to get his strawberry shortcake.

(Golden Press, $1.00)

Saggy, Baggy Elephant

Baby elephant doesn't realize he is an elephant and tries to shrink his skin because he is teased by the other animals; that is, until he finds a herd of elephants.   (Golden Press, $.29)

The Taxi That Hurried

Mother and son try to catch a train and as a result have a very frantic taxicab ride.   (Golden Press, $.29)

Tootle

Tootle, the locomotive, preferred playing in the meadow to staying on the track until the people in the town of Lower Trainswitch taught him a lesson.   (Golden Press, $.29)

FOR THE FOUR- AND FIVE-YEAR-OLDS

George Zappho,
  The Big Book of Trucks   (Grosset and Dunlap, $1.00)
  The Big Book of Trains

Does your child want to know about things that go? There are more in this series of source books for young explorers.

(Grosset and Dunlap, $1.00)

Children's Records

The following list of records was recommended to us by nursery school teachers and librarians who have found them popular with their children. Most children's records are expensive, about $4.95, but they are available at some discount stores. Many public libraries have children's records which you can borrow like books. See if yours does.

SONG AND ACTIVITY RECORDS	RECORD NO. & COMPANY	
Another Sing Along Music for movement.	#723	Young People's Records
Building a City Music for movement.	#711	Young People's Records
Let's Play Zoo Music for movement.	#802	Young People's Records
Little Indian Drum Music for movement.	#619	Young People's Records
Out of Doors Music for movement.	#724	Young People's Records
Rainy Day Music for movement.	#712	Young People's Records
Sing Along Music participation.	#722	Young People's Records
Let's Be Firemen Dramatic play.	#1024	Children's Record Guild
My Playful Scarf Rhythmic activity.	#1019	Children's Record Guild
Nothing To Do Rhythmic activity.	#1012	Children's Record Guild
Train to the Zoo Rhythmic activity.	#1001	Children's Record Guild
Visit to My Little Friend Rhythmic activity.	#1017	Children's Record Guild

Children's Songs   #TLP–1027 Tradition Records
  Sung by Ed McCurdy. A de-
  lightful album for children and
  parents.

We Wish You a Merry Christmas LP–6008 Liberty Records
  Recorded by Robert Rheims.
  Christmas favorites.

Activity Songs for Kids   #7023   Folkways
  Written and sung by Marcia
  Berman, with guitar accompa-
  niment.

Animal Songs for Children   #7051   Folkways
  Peggy Seeger sings and plays
  22 songs including "Mister Rabbit," "Peep Squirrel."

Birds, Beasts, Bugs and Little #7010   Folkways
Fishes
  Pete Seeger, with a banjo ac-
  companiment, sings "I Know an
  Old Lady," "Teency Weency
  Spider," "Skip to My Lou" and
  others. Illustrated text.

Birds, Beasts, Bugs and Bigger #7011   Folkways
Fishes
  "The Darby Ram," "The Fox,"
  and "Old Blue" are included in
  this album by Pete Seeger, with
  banjo.

Follow the Sunset   #7406   Folkways
  Nine songs from around the
  world are sung by Charity
  Bailey.

Learning as We Play   #7659   Folkways
  Songs and music for mental, so-
  cial, language and physical development.

More Learning as We Play   #7658   Folkways
  Rhythm-band activities for be-
  ginners.

More Songs to Grow On   #7009   Folkways
  Alan Mills, with guitar, sings
  "Donkey Riding," "I Ride an
  Old Paint," "Raisins and Al-
  monds," "Liza Jane," and others.

Music Time   #7307   Folkways
  Charity Bailey acts as teacher.
  Children learn to listen and
  sing with her, and make up
  songs on their own.

Sleep-time   #7525   Folkways
  Songs and stories by Pete
  Seeger include "Green Grass
  Grows All Around," "Sweet Lit-
  tle Baby," "Abiyoyo," "Sam the
  Whaler."

Songs to Grow On—Volume I: #7005   Folkways
  Nursery Days
  Sung by Woody Guthrie, this
  record includes "Put Your Finger in the Air," "Wake Up,"
  and "My Dolly."

Songs to Grow on for Mother and #7015   Folkways
  Child
  By Woody Guthrie, this album
  includes "Grow Grass," "Swim,"
  "Little Snack," "I Want Milk,"
  "I'll Eat You," and "I'll Spell a
  Word."

Muffin in the City   #601   Young People's Records
  A day in the life of a little
  black dog in the city.

Muffin in the Country   #603   Young People's Records
  A day in the life of a little
  black dog in the country.

Winnie the Pooh   #POS–1302 Pathways of Sound,
  Contains the following three   102 Mt. Auburn St.
  chapters in their entirety: "Win-   Cambridge, Mass.
  nie the Pooh," "Winnie the
  Pooh Goes Visiting—An Alto-
  gether Alarming Adventure,"
  and "Winnie the Pooh Goes
  Hunting," as read by Maurice
  Evans.

Creepy Crawly Caterpillar   #5019   Young People's Records
  Sound music

Picture Book Parade Records   #PBP101–109, Weston Woods,
  Sensitive telling of stories from   Weston, Conn.

contemporary classic children's   PBP111, 112, 144
books accompanied by original
musical scores and subtle sound
effects. Includes such favorites
as: "Make Way for Ducklings,"
"Little Toot," "Curious George
Rides a Bike," and "Three Blind
Mice."

(No "Cirderella," "Jack and the Bean Stalk," "Three Little Pigs"
records are recommended until at least five years of age.)

FOLK SONGS

Burl Ives Sings the Little White   #HL–9507 Harmony Records
Duck and Other Favorites
A collection of famous folk-
songs for children including
"The Grey Goose," "Mr. Frog-
gie Went A-Courtin," "The Sow
Took the Measles," and "Buck-
eye Jim."

Burl Ives Sings for Fun   #DL–8248 Decca
Contains such favorites as "Blue
Tail Fly," "Big Rock Candy
Mountain," and "Goober Peas."

Captain Burl Ives' Ark   #DL–8587 Decca
Animal folksongs for sing-along
or rhythmics.

American Folk Songs for Children   #7001   Folkways
Sung by Pete Seeger, after the
Fireside Book by Ruth Craw-
ford Seeger. "Jim Crack Corn,"
"Billy Barlow," and "This Old
Man" are among the selections.

Folk Songs for Young People   #7532   Folkways
Pete Seeger sings, among others,
"Blow the Man Down," "Day-
enu," and "Oh Worrycare," an
Ibo legend adapted by Pete
Seeger.

Folk Songs for Young Folk, Volume One   #7021   Folkways
Accompanied by guitar, Alan Mills sings "Alphabet Song," "A Frog He Would A-Wooing Go," "Three Little Pigs," and others.

Songs To Grow On—Volume II: *School Days*   #7020   Folkways
"The Mocking Bird," "Little Brass Wagon," and "The Grey Goose" are sung by a variety of artists.

You Can Sing It Yourself   #7624   Folkways
Twenty-three folksongs are sung by Robin Christenson. "Children, Go Where I Send Thee," "Deep Blue Sea" and "Kumbaya" are but a few of the songs. This album includes music transcripts for group participation.

MUSIC FOR FALLING ASLEEP

Beethoven	*Moonlight Sonata*
Debussy	*Clair de Lune*
	Children's Corner Suite
	Golliwog's Cake Walk
Mozart	*Eine Kleine Nachtmusik*
Smetana	*Moldau*

GOOD MUSIC TO LISTEN TO

Mozart-Haydn	*Toy Symphony*
Prokofieff	*Peter and the Wolf*
Tchaikovsky	*Nutcracker Suite*
	Overture 1812
Saint-Saëns	*Carnival of the Animals*
Bizet	*L'Arlésienne Suite*
Stravinsky	*Petrouchka*
	Firebird Suite
Ravel	*Mother Goose Suite*

MUSIC SONGBOOKS

L. F. Wood and L. B. Scott,
Singing Fun
(Webster Publishing Company, St. Louis, Mo.,
Book: $2.40; Record: $6.95)

Beatrice Landek,
Songs to Grow On
Popular songs for children. (Marks Publishing Co., $3.95.)

More Songs to Grow On
More fun children's songs. (Landek/Sloane Publishing Company,
$4.50.)

Good Ideas

FOR A CHILD WHO IS "OUT OF SORTS"

Choose quiet activities for a sick or tired child; choose vigorous things for a child who needs to let off steam.

	TODDLERS AND CRAWLERS	1-YEAR-OLDS	2- & 3- YEAR-OLDS	3-, 4-, 5- YEAR-OLDS
Alarm clock or radio	X			
A long journey through the house or yard			X	X
Bath time	X	X	X	X
Books			X	X
Building blocks				X
Coloring				X
Cornmeal sandbox			X	
Cutting magazines				X
Dancing			X	X
Fall Guy dolls			X	X
Feltboard			X	X
Finger paint				X

	TODDLERS AND CRAWLERS	1-YEAR-OLDS	2- & 3-YEAR-OLDS	3-, 4-, 5-YEAR-OLDS
Furniture play pen		X	X	
Listening to music	X	X	X	X
Milk cartons		X	X	X
Music		X	X	X
Nesting toys	X	X	X	
Newspaper fight			X	X
Pasting			X	X
Picture book without words			X	
Play dough or clay			X	X
Printing				X
Puppets				X
Puzzles			X	X
Reading aloud		X	X	X
Reserved kitchen drawer			X	X
Scribbling and painting		X	X	X
Sewing				X
Shakers made from salt containers			X	X
Shaving-soap painting			X	X
Shoe box and spools		X	X	
Singing				X
Soap bubbles			X	X
Sorting silverware, buttons, money and cards				X
Stringing buttons or macaroni				X
Tearing old sheets, paper			X	X

	TODDLERS AND CRAWLERS	1-YEAR-OLDS	2- & 3-YEAR-OLDS	3-, 4-, 5-YEAR-OLDS
Washing woodwork				X
Washing vegetables				X
Water play			X	X

OUTDOORS

	TODDLERS AND CRAWLERS	1-YEAR-OLDS	2- & 3-YEAR-OLDS	3-, 4-, 5-YEAR-OLDS
Digging		X	X	X
Mud pies		X	X	X
Outings		X	X	X
Paintbrush			X	X
Water		X	X	X

Good Ideas

WHEN A MOTHER IS "OUT OF SORTS"

	TODDLERS AND CRAWLERS	1-YEAR-OLDS	2- & 3-YEAR-OLDS	3-, 4-, 5-YEAR-OLDS
Alarm clock or radio	X			
Band or parade				X
Blanket		X	X	X
Bowling alley				X
Building			X	X
Chalk painting				X
Clothespins (old-fashioned kind)	X	X	X	X
Coloring				X
Doll house				X
Dress up				X
Empty milk cartons	X	X	X	X
Empty shoe boxes		X	X	X
Empty spools (large)	X	X	X	X

	TODDLERS AND CRAWLERS	1-YEAR-OLDS	2- & 3-YEAR-OLDS	3-, 4-, 5-YEAR-OLDS
Feltboard			X	X
Full cans and mix boxes			X	X
Listening to records		X	X	X
Magazine paper chains				X
Magazine picture book		X	X	X
Magazine pictures			X	X
Magazine puzzle			X	X
Magic markers			X	X
Mobile	X			
Nesting toys	X	X	X	
Old sheet				X
Painting on newspaper				X
Paper-bag masks				X
Pasting-picture, collage with textured materials			X	X
Percolator, metal		X	X	X
Pie plates, aluminum or tinfoil		X	X	X
Play dough			X	X
Playing store				X
Pots and lids		X	X	X
Puppets				X
Puzzles			X	X
Reserved kitchen drawer		X	X	X
Sandbox			X	X
Shaving-soap painting			X	X
Sorting silverware, cards				X
Special bag		X	X	X

	TODDLERS AND CRAWLERS	1-YEAR-OLDS	2- & 3-YEAR-OLDS	3-, 4-, 5-YEAR-OLDS
Straws and pipe cleaners				X
Stringing spools, buttons				X
Tearing sheets, newspaper				X
Train or plane trip				X
TV dinner pan	X	X	X	X
Wooden spoon	X	X	X	X

Good Ideas

FOR A GROUP OF CHILDREN

Band or parade				X
Big carton house				X
Big carton tunnel		X	X	X
Blanket house		X	X	X
Boards and crates			X	X
Building			X	X
Brush rollers				X
Cake and pie pans		X	X	
Coloring				X
Cooking				X
Cornmeal sandbox			X	X
Dancing			X	X
Dress up				X
Dusting and vacuuming				X
Empty milk cartons			X	X
Full cans and mix boxes			X	X
Furniture play area		X	X	
Kitchen help				X

	TODDLERS AND CRAWLERS	1-YEAR-OLDS	2- & 3-YEAR-OLDS	3-, 4-, 5-YEAR-OLDS
Listening to records		X	X	X
Macaroni stringing				X
Magazine paper chains				X
Magazine pictures				X
Make-believe				X
Milk-carton bowling alley				X
Music	X	X	X	X
Musical games				X
Newspaper battle				X
Painting			X	X
Paper-bag masks				X
Pasting			X	X
Play dough or clay			X	X
Playing house				X
Playing store				X
Playing train, plane				X
Pots and lids		X	X	
Printing				X
Puppets				X
Puzzles			X	X
Reading aloud		X	X	X
Sewing				X
Singing				X
Soap bubbles			X	X
Sorting buttons, silverware, cards, etc.				X
Straws and pipe cleaners				X
Table leaf and cartons		X	X	X

	TODDLERS AND CRAWLERS	1-YEAR-OLDS	2- & 3-YEAR-OLDS	3-, 4-, 5-YEAR-OLDS
Tearing paper, old sheets				X
Throwing games—ball, bean bag				X
Tin cans and old-fashioned clothespins		X	X	
Washing woodwork				X
Water play			X	X

OUTDOORS

	TODDLERS AND CRAWLERS	1-YEAR-OLDS	2- & 3-YEAR-OLDS	3-, 4-, 5-YEAR-OLDS
Blowing bubbles			X	X
Digging			X	X
Mud pies		X	X	X
Paintbrush			X	X
Outing			X	X

Further Reading for Parents

Ruth E. Hartley and Robert E. Goldenson
The Complete Book of Children's Play
A classic reference which is highly readable and full of inspiring play ideas for the child from infancy through the teen years. Expensive, but worth it.   (Thomas Y. Crowell, 1963, $6.50)

Pitcher, Lasher, Feinberg, Hammond
Helping Young Children Learn
Written for teachers by a team of child-growth experts, this fine book also is invaluable to parents wishing to introduce their children under six to art, books, music and the natural sciences.
(Merrill Publishing Co., 1966, $3.95)

Hilary Page
Playtime in the First Five Years   (J. B. Lippincott Co., $3.50)

Selma Fraiberg
The Magic Years   (Charles Scribner's, 1959, $3.95)

PAMPHLETS YOU CAN SEND FOR

Maryelle Dodds
Have Fun . . . Get Well!
(Single copies available without charge from your local branch of the American Heart Association, or write American Heart Association, 44 East 23rd St., N.Y., N.Y. 10010.)

James L. Hymes, Jr.,
Enjoy Your Child—Ages 1, 2, 3
(Public Affairs Pamphlets, 22 East 38th St., N.Y., N.Y., $.35)

James L. Hymes, Jr.
Three to Six   (Public Affairs Pamphlets, $.35)

Index

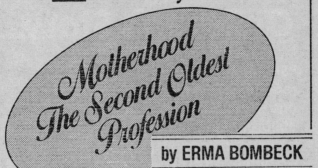

"AN IRISH <u>THORN BIRDS</u>."

LIGHT A PENNY CANDLE
by Maeve Binchy

From the moment shy Elizabeth White and bold Aisling O'Connor met as children, the girls formed a bond stronger than friendship. For two decades they were closer than sisters, supportive of each other during every crisis they faced. Until the shattering, painful moment when they realized they both loved the same man. "A sumptuous saga—war and peace, birth and death, wealth and squalor, marriage and divorce, religion, insanity, and more."—*Harper's* $3.95